The Poetry Review

The Poetry Society, 22 Betterton Street, London WC2H 9BX

The Poetry Review

The Poetry Society, 22 Betterton Street, London WC2H 9BX
Tel: +44 (0)20 7420 9883 • Fax: +44 (0)20 7240 4818
Email: poetryreview@poetrysociety.org.uk
www.poetrysociety.org.uk

Editor: Maurice Riordan
Production: Michael Sims

ISBN: 978-1-900771-90-0 ISSN: 0032 2156
Cover illustration Sarah Hanson / Début Art

. . .

SUBMISSIONS
For details of our submission guidelines,
please visit the The Poetry Review section of
www.poetrysociety.org.uk

ADVERTISING
To advertise, visit poetrysociety.org.uk
or contact Robyn Donaldson on
+44 (0)20 7420 9886,
email: marketing@poetrysociety.org.uk

BOOKSHOP DISTRIBUTION
Central Books, 99 Wallis Road, London
E9 5LN, UK. Tel: 0845 458 9925
or visit www.centralbooks.com

PBS EXCLUSIVE BOOK SUPPLY SERVICE
Readers of The Poetry Review can receive many
of the books featured in the magazine post-free
by mail order from the Poetry Book Society.
To order, tel: +44 (0)20 7831 7468,
Mon-Fri, quoting The Poetry Review.

SUBSCRIPTIONS & SALES
UK individuals: £34 / Europe: £44
Rest of the World: £49
(all overseas delivery is by airmail)
Single issue: £8.95 plus postage.
Order from www.poetryreview.org.uk or contact
Paul McGrane on +44 (0)20 7420 9881.
Pay by cheque (sterling and US dollar
cheques only), credit card or Direct Debit.

The Poetry Review is also available on audio CD.

The Poetry Review is the magazine of The
Poetry Society and was first published in 1912.
A subscription to The Poetry Review is included as
part of membership of the Poetry Society. It is also
on sale in leading bookshops. A digital version of
the magazine is also available. Views expressed in
The Poetry Review are not necessarily those of the
Poetry Society; those of individual contributors
are not necessarily those of the Editor.
Charity Commission No. 303334.

CONTENTS

Poems

Prose

Gallery

Poems

Reviews

EDITORIAL

My walk to the office often takes me past Zimbabwe House on the Strand. Invariably, I glance up at Jacob Epstein's sculptures – the eighteen primitive naked bodies that occupy its façade. They were commissioned by the British Medical Association in 1908 to adorn its new headquarters. The raw physicality of the statues caused an outcry, and drew thousands of spectators. In the 1930s, these wonderful pieces of early modernist sculpture were defaced when the building became the Rhodesian embassy. 'Defaced', though, is not quite the *mot juste*. Today none of their genital specificity remains.

Epstein's design brings to mind an era of "great, gross art", the early twentieth century that produced such scandalous works as *The Rite of Spring*, Molly Bloom's soliloquy, *Lady Chatterley's Lover*, 'Leda and the Swan'. Nowadays, it seems enviable that works of art could provoke such shock. The pornographic and blasphemous are part of everyday life, comparatively harmless phenomena alongside the depictions of violence and bestiality we can readily access. What shocks us more in the West is the intolerance of countries that still have rigid sexual and religious codes – though such societies can harbour, as we see in this issue from the example of the "landays" of illiterate Afghan women, a subversive mischievous creativity.

The capacity to shock comes up as well in Julian Stannard's tribute to Frederick Seidel, whose first book, *Final Solutions*, caused a scandal in 1963. And he has managed some notoriety since, when, for example, he spies on the Eurostar "a flock of Japanese schoolgirls ready to be fucked / In their school uniforms" – not to mention the rise in temperature when he writes,

"I hate seeing the anus of a beautiful woman... It should not be there". Seidel's ability to disturb is exceptional and currently much admired in the effort to escape the blandness of conventional writing.

I'd suggest, even so, that an offensive poem can do more than just test our sense of good taste. It should operate also in a way that is mysterious, if we let that word resonate to its deeper level of what is forbidden, occult, hidden. A small instance comes to mind from Elizabeth Bishop's 'The Filling Station'. The poem celebrates a dirty, oil-permeated wayside garage and finds in it nothing less than human redemption. It's a poem where so much depends upon a lovingly embroidered "doily" that it is repeated three times. I'd guess the unconscious mind registers that doily as a sexual emblem before one actually notices the 'oil' contained in the word.

It's often such a secret ingredient that accounts for a poem's electric effect, that static we sense on the page when we read it, or even before we read it. In the theoretical explorations of Julia Kristeva, the power of art is said to arise from the unconscious response to the "abject" on the frontier where desire is confronted with horror and disgust. Meaning emerges in a borderland "where identities... do not exist or only barely so – double, fuzzy, heterogeneous, animal, metamorphosed, altered, abject." Maybe so. At any rate, I'd say the pleasure of poems includes a sense of freedom that often involves broaching the illicit, as when those 'anonymous' Pashtun women exchange couplets in the huddle of menial labour.

However, poetry need not take the frontal route. It's as inclined to be oblique, its language subtle or coded, or liable to set off associations not consciously intended. In a later poem, 'Santarem', Bishop writes of finding at the pharmacy an exquisite empty wasps' nest, which her travelling-companion Mr Swan ("really a very nice old man") says is "ugly". But Bishop admires it so much, she is given it for free.

Maurice Riordan

MICHAEL LONGLEY

The Barnacle Geese

My friend the ornithologist
Fits barnacle geese with trackers
(Powered by the sun) fastening them
Between the wings with old-fashioned
Knicker-elastic that ties goose
To satellite – and to memories
Of handstands in the playground – June,
Helen, Mina (in spectacles) – skirts
Tucked into bulging bloomers –
For this Greenland odyssey
Until, alarmed by ash and steam
From Eyjafjallajökull,
Way up in the sky they hesitate.
From what Hebridean island
Do they scrutinise the plume,
Barnacle geese with girls' names,
Girls who kick up their sunny heels?

Fifty Years

You have walked with me again and again
Up the stony path to Carrigskeewaun
And paused among the fairy rings to pick
Mushrooms for breakfast and for poetry.

You have pointed out, like a snail's shell
Or a curlew feather or mermaid's purse,
The right word, silences and syllables
Audible at the water's windy edge.

We have tracked otter prints to Allaran
And waited for hours on our chilly throne,
For fifty years, man and wife, voices low,
Counting oystercatchers and sanderlings.

The Nosegay

Let us follow Gwen John's
Night-walk down the lanes
Picking colourless flowers,
Our nosegay of shadows,

So that, come the morning,
We wake to the surprise
Of light-painted flowers,
A field in a toothglass.

JULIA COPUS

Sunday Morning at Oscar's

I'd left the village to its farrago
of dog-walkers, devil-dodgers and kids
hurling their cries and compact bodies
skywards on the Vanderplanks'
endlessly lissom trampoline
and made for town. My catabolic nerves
had run me ragged – which is how I found myself,
goosed and fretful, pootling
among the mirrored pillars and caramel-
coloured wood panelling of Oscar's. Once again
it amazes me how quickly I may be soothed
by orderly rows of hosiery! The trick
is to give yourself up to the calm of it, the white
and the black packets, each one forward-facing, ranged
as in a child's bookcase – Oh Mr Wordsworth,
I say aloud, the world is not *enough* with us,
and am drawn immediately to the silken samples
that hang on the wall, head-height, like trophy tails and
soon I'm stretching one over my hand, and then
another, trying them for colour: *nearly nude,*
powder, noisette, illusion. I go on
up the steps to Cosmetics, and am happy there
for a good five minutes painting earnest stripes
on the back of my left hand in shades of coral
and pink (lately I'm in thrall
to my ersatz sense of otherness – praise be
for the narcissism of small differences!).
The silver lipstick boxes ranked
like terracotta soldiers lightly
joggle, lightly right themselves again
as I open the commodious drawer,
lift out a luminous *Rose Boudoir* and seeing

the tills deserted drop the packet
into my mackintosh pocket. Then how quickly
it begins to feel at home there! Nested,
like an egg. Two naked alabaster mannequins
recede behind me as I trace my steps
back over the blonde carpet. Near the exit
three shoulder bags the size of small dogs crouch,
straight out of one of my pellucid dreams,
on a low wood table, and I'm out in the street
with the pram-faces, the kooks and mavericks, lank,
slope-shouldered desperados, some of them turning
with me now into the passage of Magdalene Walk
where above us the vast, closed-petalled winds
of late mid-morning gather and I push my feet
one after the other on then on a little
quicker than usual, because it looks like rain.

JAMES GIDDINGS

The Last of the Handshakers

I am the last and I will shake everyone's hand:
the smooth, the calloused, even those with an allotment
of oniony warts sprouting at the webs of their fingers.

Who will be there, if not me, at business deals
to make pleasant with the CEOs, shake firmly on an agreement
or grease the palm of a crooked official with a bribe

cupped like an ace up a cheater's sleeve? Please,
where would the world be without *me*, the last handshaker?
Grandads would be forced into giving macho hugs

at graduations, or more embarrassingly, fist bumps:
their walnut knuckles cracking as fists collide,
the arthritic pop sounding out another broken bond –

a sturdy workmanlike pat on the back not enough
to recover from the awkwardness shooting up the arm
of the shaking hand; the pins and needles signalling

the death of its use. I have massaged my metacarpals,
gone through a bushel of apples for stress balls: now take
this offering like it's the last song to be sung. Sing it with me.

There is a Part at the End of the Film

Today we are shooting the scene where you (the villain)
cut off my hands and I (the male lead) fall hopelessly to my knees
and call for the Gods, or the police, or whatever the line is.

You are radiant in the way a high-school Mary is
in the thudding light of a broken North Star. I fumble my lines
and repeatedly drop my severed hands like a blustered Basil Fawlty.

You almost spit out your set of fake teeth as we retake
the scene, my hands screwed on backwards. I am juvenile
when I go to pray, all haphazard with my marks.

Cue a backlight of the director's scorn, his fawning cameras
keeping me less handsome. He readjusts your light. I am pummelled
by the clapperboard. Take after take I am dismembered

for his entertainment. He can see through the wooden acting.
There is a part at the end of the film where everyone is happy
and we are all forgiven for our atrocities. The orchestra plays

only good notes as your costume drains to a lighter shade.
The world is no longer mysterious.
                              Cut! The director yells,

and the day unspools like a prosthetic gut. You walk away
holding my severed hand as you would a boyfriend's. I watch
to make sure you don't let go, throw what's left of me in the bin.

A Small Windswept Town

I would like to make a town. It could be
anywhere in the world; but it might as well
be in Britain where an old man's loud,
sharp cough drops like a stone and breaks
on the concrete. Miners might stand strung out
along the road like bunting, or crouch
on the corner with bait boxes, shivering
against a cold wall of wind. The cows
might thread their route through the grazing
fields on their way back from the milking sheds.
And every house would stand like its own
oil lamp, bright and warm, with attics full
of sunlight, the smell of apples. The chimneys
would yawn and the stairs would moan
with weight, but there will be blossoms
on the gravestones and the poor shrieking
night-bird will bring comfort. Everything
will be local, even happiness in his yellow coat
will be there, unflinching and stoic, politely
refusing the rain his place at the bus stop.

TIM LIARDET

Cop Convo, Subtitles Only

This is my road, says the cop, this the next bend yawning.
This is my road that goes on and on.
I can swing around my long lazy Dodge any time I choose
and come after you. I can do what I want.

You act like you do what you choose, she says, like this
is your road. This the immaculate camber
from which you scrape the squashed skunk.
You sweep, you scrape. You need to keep it swept.

I pull you over, he says, you have on your fog-lamps
and there is no fog. Those filaments hot with brilliance
while all your other lights are off, though it is dark.
Most people keep on their lights in the dark.

Most people, she says, keep on all their lights.
I prepare always for an arcane weather.
The particles of darkness are another sort of fog. I probe
another sort of dark. You do not know which sort.

This, he says, is my lamp's blue hysteria, encased in a bottle,
it is the light which beats harder the more I catch up.
Law, she says, is what burns the night blue,
our faces bluer. I wish your fog-lamps fog.

HELEN MORT

Ablation

Inside the Northern General
they're trying to burn away
a small piece of your heart.

I want to know which bit,
how much
and what it holds.

My questions live
between what doctors call the heart
and what we mean by it,

wide as the gap between brain and mind.
And in our lineage of bypassed hearts
we should be grateful

for the literal. I know my heart
is your heart – good for running,
not much else

and later as you sit up in your borrowed bed
I get the whole thing wrong,
call it *oblation*. Offering

or sacrifice. As if you'd given something up.
As if their tiny fire was ritual
and we could warm by it.

MIKE BARLOW

Ill Wind

There's no end to where it's been, nor
where it's going, it brings the far-flung
in its salts and sands – germs and minute
splinters garnered continents away,
the reek and debris of a hundred wars.

There's no end to its curses either,
imprecations of the damned, barbed gossip
from both enemy and friend,
the prating of the righteous
invoking all God's names at once.

It likes to play the final angel, list
your misdeeds one by one, weigh your soul
and find you wanting. But this
you knew already and any news it brings
you've heard before, headlined and edited.

It's no news that's the good news, as they say,
descending like sudden silence on a crowd
one clear unforecast windless winter day.

JEMMA BORG

Quickening

My son in his ancient world is swallowing dreams
while my heartbeat entangles him

and he coils at my navel, the pendulums
of his legs accruing bone and his soft hands

shuddering at his face as he gulps at seawater.
He is, for this short time, a saint

getting ready to fall from concealment.
His heel quivers: the body wakes upon jerking strings.

Tiny snake-soul: you are the first strong child
to stir in me, and stay bound.

The globe of your head settles deeper at my pelvis.
When they lift you out of me, you ascend

in the too-bright light, your head black with blood,
your toes like grains of cooked rice and you curl

in on yourself like a coral, the quenelle
of your back gleaming. And then, your cry goes up

in astonished multiplication
and, before they sew me shut with wire, it breaks

the year open and enters me
                with its candelabra of vowels.

JODIE HOLLANDER

He's

just about the size of a goldfish
and doesn't even look like a child.
When did he arrive? I don't remember –
the pain must have made me forget.
Anyway, now I have a son
that lives in my cupped-together hands
in a small pool of water I think he needs.
I spend my hours closely watching him,
nervous he'll slip between my fingers
and vanish down some drain forever,
or worse, he'll try and swim away.

Each day he gets a little bigger,
'til he no longer needs my hands.
I carry him around like a baby,
buy him PJs with yellow ducks,
and little booties to keep his feet warm.
He smells like the sweetness of a baby
and smiles at me, I cautiously smile back.
Now he's growing faster by the hour –
and I can no longer handle the weight.
My arms start to tire – *I must tell him.*
I put his soft cheek on mine, and say
he simply cannot grow any bigger,
he must promise me to always stay small –
so that I know I can love him.

RUBY ROBINSON

Apology

I can't go up because I don't know how.
Nobody has shown me.

So many names, my mother, I'm never sure
what to call you. So many names for all your predators
and crushes and suitors. I'm sorry.

I'm sorry I'm here and I'm sorry I'm not here.
Would you have made it on your own
without the comorbid condition of motherhood
and the slowness and consistency of time?

I'm sorry for the slowness and consistency of time;
years like zombies dawdling towards a cliff edge
holding back the child's writhing body, itching to grow, packed
around the same mind I have now.

I'm sorry the concept of promise outgrew the concept of child
and that systemic contradiction and wizardry left only a dim sense
of suspicion; a crescending breeze, accumulating clouds
amidst bewildering dichotomies.

I'm sorry for resembling your relatives and captors and the man
who penetrated you, who's still there, communicating boldly
via intersections of others' thought waves and memories,
blatant into the long nights, haunting,

for my inferiority in the face of nuclear family culture,
feeding on detritus of white goods, leisure sports, laminate floors,
a real home and fake recycling,

for creeping by night into a tight void, blinds down, brain blown
glass-thin, electric impulses and bloated thoughts bolted in.
For this life being the only one my quiet mind knows,

   its many versions and phases, I'm sorry. I wasn't your daughter
   – or anyone – when you were the blue-water navy,
   or the beheaded, or the baby boy. Or was I?

I'm sorry I was not yet born and could not yet hear you
      when you were over there, listening carefully
      for the rain and small movements of animals, for sounds
      of life, through a green, five-fingered haze.

I'm sorry I consider sentiment, fact; authenticity, originality,
      when they are irrelevant. So many choices
      in supermarkets, the natural habitat of panic attacks, it's enough
      to make anyone sorry and I am.

I'm sorry it's taking more than half a century to link your purple-patched
      brain scan to the basic biology of stress. The piano thunders on,
      sustain pedal wired to the facial muscles of all your neglecters,
      aching like hell behind their stamina and machinery.

I'm sorry I had, logically, to think of my own self first/simultaneously,
      navigating through the fire and acid of Trust and her sycophant Love
      before returning. All the powerful were women; even the power
      of penises and facial hair originated there, cajoled by matriarchs.

   As if skin and breath were insignificant!
I'm so sorry.
      Where are you now, to take into my arms and resuscitate?
      Is it too late, given you're fifty and no longer a child?
      It's always mothers and mind control which is why

I thank you for breaking the cycle, withstanding the enormity
    of generations, magnetic as water,
    to let us go. You weren't to know

    about other outrageous families and sadistic counterparts.
    A nugget of my limbic system remembered choosing my own
    lemon-yellow baby clothes so thank you.

    I squeezed that into the thumb-sized space
    in the palm of my hand knowing all along they were wrong
    and imploding with it.

I'm sorry I wept in the shower for your cancelled wedding,
    letting the violet dress down the plughole, unsure what it all meant except
    things staying the same, the concept of future aggravating my brain,
    my baby brother gone again.

I'm sorry you were out there, alone, defined by the worst
    of others and defined by your children's prisms of hope
    and survival mechanisms. In one version, you did marry and lived
    in a house with green walls and extravagant furniture.

I'm sorry that consensus reality had you set fire to your bed
    as you lay in it; arrested, put in a cell, let off the next day
    because the lawyer believed it was a genuine attempt
    and convinced the police.

I'm sorry you've had to withstand such torrents
    of knowledgeless advice and legal toxification,
    clinging to reality by a sinew of tooth, remembering yourself,
    through the rough and the smooth.

I'm sorry I was absent, memorising books of the Bible
    for a bar of Dairy Milk, owning up to things
    I'd never done, getting Confirmed as an antidote
    to the evil core of me.

I'm sorry it was exotic to think of kids like me
    ending up in prison, coincidentally, inevitably
    or prevented (which is the same), salvaged, peristalsised
    through Society, brain safely contained,

    doused daily in cold water or electricity
    or disgrace, temptations kept consistently far enough away
    as to appear illusory

    like you, my brave mother, fantastic prodigy
    in flowing white kaftan, knotted long brown hair, a beautiful gaze
    of solemnity, rare stone, emotionless (defined by others).

I'm sorry I was ill-prepared for your soiled mattress
    and comatose body, under a wave of advocaat and transistor radios
    oozing with cheap Scotch. Even I developed feelings for them
    amidst adults acting like it's okay

    to leave you this way, the bluebottle flies in on it,
    inflated with dog shit and red hot egos, resting on your cheek,
    your lip, too cunning to get rid of.

I'm sorry that laughing off a difficult childhood
    didn't make it never happen. Even a basic calculator
    recognises an infinite loop as a malfunction; don't they see that *cutting off*
    my privates every night needs additional information?

I'm sorry I talked you out of wounding yourself
    although I know it feels hopeful and lets in sunlight and air
    through an open door. I'm sorry I can't help you go up.
    I, also, don't know how.

I'm sorry I prioritise the stimulation of adrenalin and opioids
    in my own axis before I come to you. Thank you
    for believing I love you even though you know
    I don't know love or trust it.

    I dreamed someone else's baby died from kidney failure. The worst part?
    Not knowing distress from relief in the face of the mother,
    like a child in an experiment. What does this mean?

    My man fearing a moment of madness. Not locking
    the knives away but keeping a steady eye on them, paying attention
    to the moon and turning moods. He underestimates me;

    I'm my own doppelgänger. Here I am, locked to him, discussing
    sex positions and holiday destinations. Here I am courting solitude
    in the doorway, a pair of eyes and a chest cavity thrumming

    on the dark boundary between survival, entertainment and self-control.
    While there are no babies, I carry on. I am testament to the problem
    of the baby. Look at me – flaunting my own survival. Who am I?

    Except the parasite that accidentally caught on
    to your womb wall as you lay stoned on a fur-lined coat
    in a hallway in Moss Side? *Happy accident, intentional accident, accidentally*

    on purpose. Close the piano lid. Empty a drawer. Things happen.

I'm sorry for absences, holidaying in France, studying guilt,
    time-travelling the pain barrier, intent on nerve endings
    and their connections to various biological systems.
    Learning to accept and relinquish responsibility appropriately.

    Throwing back the hot stone in a horizontal line.

Thank you to the policeman who took all the men whose safety you feared for
    to the pub for a meal so you could come home
    for dinner, monologue, nail varnish remover, a set
    of impartial weighing scales and cheap French wine.

I'm sorry about the home, the wine, cut glass, the monologue resonating
    against the plastic mug others might keep for you, fussing over make-up-
    smeared walls, upholstery and understatements. *I'm a bit sad*
    we can't see Al. He comes on the radio sometimes.

I'm sorry I'm not bringing you home, finally, to thrive and repair.
    I wanted to stay, singing Luther Vandross on the walkway
    outside at 6am, fetching toast from the neighbour. I was hoping
    for perfection, *believing in anything*, all those years.

    Is it too ambitious to hope? I'm sentimentally sorry
    despite a genuine fear of sentimentality and pseudo-unhappiness,
    struggling under the weight of an A1 poster on complex trauma

    and a pair of Sennheiser headphones to lock me in. *Think of*
    what it is when God himself puts his arms around you and says
    welcome home. There's nothing mysterious about my thoughts

    or affect, nor yours, nor anyone's, biologically generated
    by the relationships we try to hide our consciousness from.
    Oh unhappiness and infidelity! Disguised in metaphor

you're nothing but the deep yearning of an infant for its mother
    and the furiousness of it. Making this connection is like remembering
    being born, which is like folding time, which is no one to blame and
all the world to blame.

Thank you for picking up the handless, footless doll
    in the park, saving him from a dog or fox or thoughtless children,
    keeping him to your breast on the tram, the bus, in pubs
    and not noticing the scathing looks.

    I learnt to trust without you, leaving my thoughts
    outside for five minutes and trusting the neighbour's cat
    not to urinate on them.

I'm sorry my stand-in mother was an evil replica, machine-like
    yet unpredictable. We tried to calculate an algorithm
    for her mood, as you would've done, and in fourteen years never cracked it.
    She remained seated when I left for the last time.

You weren't to know
    and they wouldn't have believed you anyway.
    We learn to accept the clouds for what they are
and wait, patiently.

POETS READING

An occasional series in which poets write about their current reading

. . .

Bogeyman – Julian Stannard on Frederick Seidel

I came to Seidel rather late. The friend who slipped me *Ooga-Booga* said, "I think you'll like this". He was right. I even liked the title – voodoo-istic, body-swaying, tantalisingly rhythmic. Forget salsa, I wanted a little Ooga-Booga: "I am civilised, but I see the silence" ('Kill Poem'). Frederick Seidel was born in 1936, into wealth and privilege, a poet in the lap of luxury – there's a thing. When I signed up I took the habitual vow of poverty, the unheated garret, the cheque in the post. I don't wear Savile Row suits and nor do I write poems about the Four Seasons Ritz Hotel in Lisbon ("I have to say / I've had a pleasant stay"), and not a word about Ducati motorcycles. And never will I write a poem about Diane Von Furstenburg. Which is why I'm pleased that Seidel does. The American patrician, and Jew, with his eagle-nest view of Broadway – both somehow an insider and an outsider – may well be part of some Faustian pact: the epicurean who name-drops more than Robert Lowell, this is gossip of the highest order, and blessed with such wayward gifts. I want to know what happens in the final scene. Or maybe Dantean is the more apposite term.

There are glimpses of a hedonistic dissolute paradise (I am reminded of Paolo Sorrentino's *The Great Beauty*), but Seidel is particularly good at hell. He is the undisputed master of the "disagreeable poem" and, rather like the shark which has a particular evolutionary role, his poetry is both disturbing and functional – "What could be more pleasant than talking about people dying [?]", he asks in 'For Holly Andersen', where "Dr Holly Andersen has a vodka cosmopolitan, / And has another, and becomes positively Neapolitan". He has been called "the poet the twentieth century deserved". Now we are in the twenty-first century – late capitalism spewing out grotesquery with incontinence, the undeserving rich forever in our midst – we need him more than ever. He both fetishises the trappings of wealth and is seemingly revolted by them.

Beholden to no one, a poet who neither does readings nor promotes his work, a poet outside the Academy, a poet who need not genuflect to any Mission Statement, Seidel can write about anything with two urbane fingers to the world. He has put a bomb under the lingering notion of the poetic subject. And being more than happy to offend he is, necessarily, a divisive figure. When he wrote "A naked woman my age is a total nightmare" ('Broadway Melody'), there were howls of protest, and it seems certain, even as he was writing the poem, that he was enjoying the opprobrium: "It doesn't matter. One doesn't care. / One doesn't say it out loud because it's rare / For anyone to be willing to say it, / Because it's the equivalent of buying a billboard space to display it."

Ange Mlinko accuses Seidel of employing "the prosody of atrocity" – see, for example, his holocaust poem 'Mr Delicious', where the poet *inter alia* rhymes "campfire goo" with "Gooey Jew". David Orr has compared Seidel to "a violinist who pauses from bowing expertly through Paganini's Caprice no. 24 to smash his instruments against the wall [...] Such a combination of barbarity and grace is one of Seidel's most remarkable achievements." Billy Collins, it seems to me, hits the nail on the head, and this is why I embrace Seidel wholeheartedly: "He does what every exciting poet must do: avoid writing what everyone thinks of as 'poetry'". In *Where Have You Been? Selected Essays* (2015), Michael Hofmann calls Seidel (approvingly) "a bogeyman". The American, he continues, is "a carnivore if not a cannibal in the blandly vegan compound of contemporary poetry". Seidel is wondrously devoid, in fact, of any "pissy beauty". Consider, for example, the second stanza of 'To Die For': "The little black specks were

Frederick Seidel portrait © Adam Graff 2015

shipped to Brazil in ships. / The Portuguese whipped the little black specks to bits. / The sugar plantations on the horrible tropical coast where the soil was rich / Were a most productive ant Auschwitz."

Seidel fell foul of the Poetry Police at the very beginning. His first collection – *Final Solutions* (1963) – was awarded a prize offered by the 92nd Street YMHA. The committee subsequently rejected the manuscript on the grounds of anti-Semitism, anti-Catholicism and obscenity. Controversy from the start, the perfect way to start one's career.

'Bologna' begins "My own poetry I find incomprehensible". 'Racer' begins "I spend most of my time not dying. / That's what living is for. / I climb on a motorcycle. / I climb on a cloud and rain. / I climb on a woman I love. / I repeat my themes." 'Fog' begins in exactly the same way – an identical opening stanza – and proceeds: "Here I am in Bologna again / Here I go again. / Here I go again, getting happier and happier." Hofmann, in fact, considers Seidel's (seemingly cavalier) technical genius – the repetitions, obsessions, devil-may-care relocations, entire lines moving from poem to poem as if he were spoiling or perhaps enhancing the aura of the individual piece: "The lines are stuff, material, mortadella, it doesn't greatly matter. The poet is a meat-slicing machine." Material is worked, re-worked, sliced, the wheat deliberately contaminated by the chaff, the lyrical gesture negotiated, beautifully attenuated:

> The Lord is my shepherd and the Director of Superbike Racing.
> He buzzes me through three layers of security
> To the innermost secret sanctum of the racing department
> Where I will breathe my last.
> Trains are delayed.
> The Florence sky is falling snow.

The "Laureate of the Louche", a combination of dandyism and Dada, the supremely talented sardonic prankster. The late Romantic schooled by French Symbolism, by Ezra Pound (in part), by Lowell (in plenty): think Prufrock and Edward Lear with loads of pharmaceutical zest. Seidel's Jewishness is not insignificant. He is an astutely political poet. He writes about savagery and cruelty with knockabout savagery and cruelty (the poem is a biting machine, its pseudo-infantile rhymes are full of teeth).

Alvarez called for a poetic which recognised the reality of twentieth-century "mass evil" (*The New Poetry*, 1962). Seidel is mindful, clearly, of

Theodor Adorno's much discussed (and much glossed) dictum: "No lyric Poetry after Auschwitz". Seidel's anti-lyricism (he provides gorgeous poetic interludes) is aesthetically and ideologically congruous, ultimately a way of saving poetry from itself. Poetry which doesn't seem like *poetry*. From 'Kill Poem':

> Our only decision was how to cook the venison.
> I am civilised but
> I see the silence
> And write the words for the thought-balloon.
> When the woods are the colour of a macaroon,
> Deer, death is near.
> I write about its looks in my books.
> I write disappearing scut.
> I write rut.

> The title is *Kill Poetry*,
> And in the book poetry kills.
> In the poem the stag at bay weeps, literally.
> Kill poetry is the *hallali* on Avenue Paul-Valéry.
> Get rid of poetry. Kill Poetry.
> Label on a vial of pills. Warning: Kill kill kill kills.
> Its title is *Kill Poem*,
> From the *Book of Kills*.
> The antlered heads are mounted weeping all around the walls.

> John F. Kennedy is mounted weeping on the wall.

Apart from 'Mr Delicious', the poems referred to can be found in Ooga-Booga (2006). Collected Poems 1959–2009 was published in 2009. Julian Stannard delivered a short talk on Seidel's 'Il Duce' at the Aldeburgh Poetry Festival 2014: 'More than one woman at a time / Is the policy that got the trains running on time.'

Sarah Howe on Peter Streckfus

I spent my childhood in Hong Kong hearing my mother speak a language I couldn't understand. With its eight tones, Cantonese seemed peculiarly close to music, to the singsong of English nursery rhymes looping on cassettes in the car. I sometimes wonder if that experience left me more susceptible to language as sound and cadence, separated from sense.

What exactly is Chinese about Chinese Whispers? I was perplexed and beguiled by this question as a child. Americans call it Telephone, the children's game with cumulative and even wilful error at its heart. Some would do away with the phrase, freighted as it is with the notion that foreigners speak meaningless nonsense – mere sound, like the jingle of "Ching Chong Chinaman" I met for the first time, aged eight, in an English school playground.

The strange and inexorable logic of Chinese Whispers imbues both collections by the American poet Peter Streckfus. They have the feel of allegories, but allegories unconnectable back to their original, whispered message. I fell in love with his first book, *The Cuckoo* (2004), after stumbling across it a few years ago. The back cover hails its eccentric melding of American and Chinese culture as "an impossible combination of John Ashbery and Ezra Pound". (That would be some love-child.) In fact, Streckfus attains an air of Zen-like mysticism quite alien to both, doggedly skirting rationality by means both lyrical and ludic. The final line of one poem, 'After Words', crystallises into a sort of *ars poetica*: "I'll speak nonsense. You speak truth. We'll see what comes of it."

I read Streckfus's second book, *Errings* (2014), for the first time this summer. It turns out it's a patchier volume than his exquisite first, though some of its more directly autobiographical sections are simply and intensely moving. 'Bildungsroman' obliquely recalls the drowning of two older sisters, having slipped out a back gate, in a canal near their house. This trauma occurred before the poet's own birth, but still twangs in the anxious bodies of his parents: "Who could we be to you, we who you never knew, your siblings – we who / could not swim until adulthood." The title poem has more in common with *The Cuckoo*'s unsteady terrain, premised as it is on a Chinese Whispers-like linguistic divagation. 'Errings' is a winding, compressed, deteriorated epic that adapts language from the unpublished typescript of *Two Golden Earrings*, a rollickingly absurd pirate adventure written by the poet's father, Robert Streckfus, when he was a young Catholic monk in Peru. By a progress of mishearings as tangential as the plot, "Earrings" (hearings?) eventually blur into the titular "Errings".

That word says a lot about Streckfus's work, which isn't afraid to embrace 'error' – a Surrealism born of felicitous slip-ups – but error too in its etymological sense of 'wandering'. Many of his poems stage quests without discernible objects, whose point is not the destination but the way. Published a decade earlier, *The Cuckoo* is similarly dominated by the mythic motif of the journey. Its anarchic and otherworldly poems overlay the spiritual pilgrimage of the monk Hsüan-tsang, who crossed Asia to receive the Buddhist Scriptures from India, with an entirely different continent and historical period – the drive to colonise the New World – somehow harmonising the two. Both archetypal journeys point towards a rumoured Western land. The final long poem, 'The Organon', is a mash-up alternating language taken from *Journey to the West* – the sixteenth-century Chinese novel that tells the story of Hsüan-tsang and his disciple Monkey (a beloved fixture of my childhood picturebooks!) and Francis Parkman's *The Oregon Trail*, with its tales of the nineteenth-century American pioneers. Like the cuckoo, Streckfus has no qualms about laying in others' nests.

Most bizarrely of all, thrown into this mix of free-floating signifiers are imagined scenes from the life of US President Ronald Reagan. According to the poems' bleary dream-logic, he sometimes morphs into an ancient Chinese emperor who had his favourite concubine brutally killed – a murder that haunts the long central poem, 'Event'. It sounds like it really shouldn't work, but it does:

Why is there a woman and not a man? Why is there not a child?
Great banquet in Heaven, you see
                                        how little there is to offer?

The woman at the edge of the field is the center of his
story: an emperor's.

The president's most loved was whipped to death with the branch of
a litchee. A pause in our journey,
                              Pilgrim Sun, fiery monkey of
stone that these our stories orbit, does a quick cloud somersault and
passes from sight.

These poems speak in a voice of resonant mystery, detached yet tender, its perspectives uncannily disembodied as though no longer exactly human. "The case for nonsense is not the same as the case against meaning," wrote Louise Glück in her preface to *The Cuckoo*, which she chose for the Yale Series of Younger Poets. "Listen to the babe-scare cry of the wind," Streckfus continues in 'After Words': "You are in the unsteady boat and this poem is a lake [...] Come on now, you have no choice. Trust me." Despite the wacky caprice of his subject matter, I find it impossible not to accept that proffered hand.

Sometimes the poems float into other consciousnesses like a trans-migrating soul, their tone still recognisable, but temporarily inhabiting a tree, or bird, or goat. One lovely poem speaks in the voice of a dung pile:

> The varied voices of crows rose and fell. As I lay in the grass, dark-eyed juncos flew down beside me,
>
> flittering and twittering, and gleaned the mustard seed fallen onto my body. Their black beads and death hoods.
>
> Their white coat tails. I whispered to them: Surely it is you who make the honey of which the Berber speak [...]
> ('The Dung Pile')

Perhaps surprisingly, for all Streckfus's postmodern hi-jinks there is enormous emotion here – heartbreak even – lodged in poems whose feel for image is as fine as their music: "One picked / out an oat seed, another, a blade of bluestem."

It's partly this empathetic extension into other lives and worlds, however alien, that I so value in Streckfus. He is no mindless tourist of the exotic, but a subtle and ethically minded explorer of what it means to imagine across the boundaries of culture and race. The first poem in the book, 'The English', invents a short, riddling dialogue between Defoe's Crusoe and Friday, restaging that colonial encounter between 'civilised' and 'savage':

> Crusoe: A bee.
> Friday: Bee?
> C: Aye, a bee.
> F: Bee...

C: Aye.
later...
C: City.
F: Cee Dee
C: City.

('The English')

By accident or intuition, Friday's nonsense displays a wisdom beyond his tutoring in the rudiments of the English alphabet. His accented "mispronunciations" open a window onto the textures and opacities of our language: what is the relationship between letters and words and sounds? Can we ever finally peer through words to their meanings? Crusoe can't step back to appreciate this insight.

The Cuckoo had me from its very first page – an epigraph that alters a single word in Nobuyuki Yuasa's translation of a haiku by Bashō:

Turn the head of your horse
sideways across the field
to let me hear
the cry of the *hototogisu.*

By untranslating the "cuckoo" of Bashō's final line, Streckfus teaches us how to read the rest of the book named in its honour. In Japanese, *hototogisu* is also onomatopoeic, at once naming the bird and mimicking its song. We hear its accents afresh, newly unfamiliar, through the ears of another culture – *hototogisu, hototogisu* – a mantra against sense. I think of a well-known koan attributed to the Zen master Zhaozhou (778–897): "Does a dog possess Buddha Nature?" "No," comes back the ritual answer, the Chinese character for negation or emptiness (無). That is, until the disciple notices the pun: the character's Japanese pronunciation is "Mu", which also happens to be that language's equivalent of "Woof!" – the onomatopoeic rendering of a dog's bark. "Emptiness," replies the dog in his own doggy tongue. In the best way, Streckfus's poems remind me of Philip Whalen's saying that poetry, like the koan, should "wreck the mind".[1]

1. *See Jonathan Stalling,* Poetics of Emptiness: Transformations of Asian Thought in American Poetry *(Fordham University Press, 2010), p. 99.*

The Cuckoo *(Yale University Press, 2004);* Errings *(Fordham University Press, 2014).*

Mark Waldron on Jeff Hilson

Here is the beginning of a poem from Jeff Hilson's 2009 collection *Bird bird*:

> Must work without the wren their shiny coats there their fat small
> hands. They once were kind. Once they all faced the same way and
> sang. Once. Doubtful bird you have seen. The word that the wren
> said: "shoes!" A wren doesn't cost any money.
> ('Troglodytes troglodytes (wren)')

I sometimes think of poems in terms of whether or not they were worth
the price of admission (a horrible expression, I know – I promise never to
use it again). Often, for me, a single phrase can be so arresting that even
if everything else in the poem is dull, I'll forgive it. Hilson manages to get
three images into those three lines, each of which would have been worth
the price of admission (oops) to me: the "fat small hands", "they all faced
the same way and sang" and "A wren doesn't cost any money." Each of
those ideas has an absolutely delicious degree of absurdity that makes me
feel a tiny bit sick with happiness.

There's an absurdist quality to Hilson's poetry that brings to mind
Victorian English nonsense writing, a nonsensical quality arising out
of its use of unlikely juxtapositions, found elements, non-sequiturs and
intentional misspellings. There's also a peculiarly English kind of reserve
in these poems, in their passivity, in their sense of a droll resignation in
the face of a world without real meaning.

But Hilson's poetry isn't just particularly English in its humour and
tone, it often refers to England directly. Many of the poems I mention here
refer to specific places in England, or creatures or vegetation native to
England. There's a cosy familiarity set against the experimental syntax
and punctuation. It seems to me there's a kind of Monty Python-esque
view of Englishness and class that is both exposing and, at the same time,
quintessentially English itself. I think Jeff Hilson's work, and the absurdity
in it, is connected to that strain of surreal humour:

> I fucking love you months
> January & February happily

together March & April
on their own & the smaller ones
May, June & obvious July.
August is very rare
we have to ask what happened
to August in September &
delicately. October there is
nothing to be said for
which like all fashions changes.
Months can be used to remember
like November November I
fucking love you sonnets

('25', *In The Assarts*)

Another aspect of the humour comes from the exaggeratedly naive voice often in conjunction with an arcane knowledge of the subject of the poem. In fact, many of the poems make use of specialist lexicons belonging to particular jobs or activities – ornithology or architecture or the ancient lore of the forest. They mean among other things to gently puncture the absurdities of that kind of technical jargon by removing it from its context and setting it down somewhere unfamiliar. In his collection *In The Assarts*, Hilson uses the sonnet form and esoteric terminology from the past combined with the fractured language, the use of ampersands and the partly absent punctuation of twentieth-century American linguistic innovation, as well as a comically banal, parochial Englishness, such as in the reference to "the common market" in the poem below. There's something just right about the combination of a kind of Larkin-esque English mundanity with the American avant-garde – to me that's very funny in itself. Much British avant-garde poetry feels like American avant-garde poetry that happens to be written over here. Hilson's poetry makes use of the absurdity in the Old World's appropriation of the New World's rebellion against it. Again this poem is a cake crammed with raisins – little moments of exquisite absurdity:

If I say a little about the timber
sorry I am become all flora interruptus.
I am tiny & exotic.
I am incapable.

I got the painless mumps
but I got you babe where we are
up in this famous ancient tree.
On my early map look over
there is our anti-highwayman trench.
Let's gamekeep our own wood.
You be holly I'm a nut.
Later in the common market he died
not being shy storming
her world where he & forgot beautiful old rhyme.

('11 (for Tim Atkins)', *In The Assarts*)

I used to think I was most drawn to poets who were doing what I couldn't do. Now I think I'm most attracted to writers who are pursuing the same thing as me, but in some different way. When I was first shown the Dream Songs, I thought, "Oh no! Someone's already done it! He's said exactly what I wanted to say! I might as well pack up now." It was like being Scott arriving at the South Pole and finding Roald Amundsen's snack wrappers scattered about. Or more like putting on my snowshoes at base camp before setting off for the South Pole and seeing Roald's snack wrappers blowing back past me out of the snowy wilderness. I read an interview with the fabulous American poet D.A. Powell. He said when he first came across Frank O'Hara he thought, "this guy's ripping me off. Except he died when I was three." It seems to me Jeff Hilson's doing not what I do, but some peculiar version of what I'd like to do. It's inimitable, at least for me, but in the mixture of the arcane and the demotic and the post-modern it captures something I sometimes aim for:

chinese marvin gaye is silly
he doesn't know what's going on

('organ music')

What I like there, I think, is that chinese marvin gaye actually is silly! As in, it's a silly thing to say as well as he being silly himself because he doesn't know what's going on:

...dear sir there were
these 3 dots which could

sing one did not say he
was free one did not say
a bar and a dog which
carry its shit by as a hobby
was made up of three dots
in a line (the difference in
a line and a dot is a line
is not shit & did not invent
sue lawley (ha ha the ur
sonata) I am in love with
steak and am a genius dot
dot dot

('stretchers volume 3 no 15')

Jeff Hilson is perceived by some in the poetry world as being in a kind of self-imposed exile on the rocky island of the avant-garde where a huddle of miserable, angry poets grumble about their state of exclusion and the bourgeois values of their tormentors, the mainstream, forgetting that they're actually ensconced there as voluntarily as any sunburnt British sunbather on a Majorcan beach. That's not an accurate picture, of course, and borders between the experimental and mainstream are thankfully beginning to blur. When I think about Hilson, however, I think of him partly in those terms – but as a kind of cheerful misfit on that island, perhaps someone who happened to get on the wrong boat, but was too kind or polite to say so, for fear of hurting the feelings of the other passengers (I'm certain he wouldn't see it that way, but I'm sticking with my story).

I'm going to end with the very funny, yet somehow also tragic opening section of 'A FALSE BOTANIC-FORENSIC POEM FOR FEBRUARY'. When it came to writing this essay I discovered I wasn't sure what it was I was drawn to in Hilson's work, but perhaps now I think the main thing I admire is that it is both experimental and accessible. At least there's a powerful feeling that comes off it that is accessible to me:

As I walked out in the morning on the first day looking for the early gentian I didnt find it in the morning instead I found an allis shad did you mean to search for an allis shad & all in the morning on the first day & as I set off in the evening on the second day to seek the creeping marshwort I didnt find it with a lantern instead I found a speckled footman I didnt mean to search for a speckled footman with a lantern or in the evening & taking a turn on the third day in the afternoon I tried to find the three lobed crowfoot I didnt find it instead in the afternoon I found axl rose I was trying to find a three lobed crowfoot instead I found axl rose & I began to cry & as I roved out early one day searching for a slender naiad it was on the fourth day & I didnt find it instead I found a narrow headed ant it was on the fourth day & I didnt find it even though I tried & on the fifth day at sunrise I went abroad looking for a lundy cabbage its just a cabbage I thought & I didnt find it I couldnt see one anywhere

stretchers *(Reality Street, 2006)*; Bird bird *(Landfill, 2009)*; In The Assarts *(Veer Books, 2010)*. *'organ music' was published in* summer stock, *issue 7 (Summer 2013)*. *'A FALSE BOTANIC-FORENSIC POEM FOR FEBRUARY' was published in* Litmus *no. 1 (April 2014)*.

Essay

EARWORMS: THE LANDAYS OF AFGHAN WOMEN

Sophie Collins

In UK poetry culture, translations are broadly conceived of as pertaining to one of two strands; 'faithful' translations that reproduce inasmuch as is possible the source text, requiring nothing more complex than a balancing of sound and sense on the part of the translator (whatever that is imagined to mean); and 'free adaptations' or 'versions', often rendered by poets with no initial knowledge of the source language, and no apparent desire to become acquainted with ongoing discussions in translation theory. Fundamentally, there is nothing wrong with either of these modes. But that our perception of translation consists, on the one hand, of the translator's approximation of the perceived original, and, on the other, of the poet's allegedly more creative and intuitive approach, is cause for concern. Such a two-pronged construction downplays or disguises the translation process (as distinct from 'versioning'), equating it to a kind of literary service that simply facilitates access to foreign texts. Consequently, the translator is rendered invisible. Her expertise and influence, down to the level of her sourcing of foreign texts, is grossly underestimated, as is every subsequent decision. Through each stage of the translation process, the choices made by the translator inscribe a particular interpretation (comprising a poetics and set of political beliefs) into the translated text.

So, if a translation can be said to be the sum of the translator's choices, what do we know of Eliza Griswold's choices in *I Am the Beggar of the World*, a collection of landays from contemporary Afghanistan? To begin with, Griswold is highly visible throughout, though this might seem like less of a choice, and more of a default property of a translation with no stable source text. Landays – couplets made up of two hemistiches (incomplete or imperfect lines of verse) – are an exclusively oral tradition in Afghanistan. The currency of the illiterate, they are most often exchanged like jokes or earworms among the twenty-million-plus Pashtun women who occupy the border between Afghanistan and Pakistan. They read like this:

Daughter, in America the river isn't wet.
Young girls learn to fill their jugs on the Internet.

and

I tried to kiss you in secret but you're bald
and your bare skull bumped against the wall.

Another:

Without the Taliban,
Afghanistan would be London.

The landays are grouped according to theme ('Love', 'Grief and Separation', and 'War and Homeland'), and are parenthesised by Griswold's accounts of her conversations with the women she met in Afghanistan, from whom she retrieved most of the book's landays first-hand (others came from "important collections or folktales", or from the Pashto Landay Facebook page). There are also explanatory notes following the majority of the landays, elucidating aspects of Afghan culture and the poems' more oblique references, so that we might better understand them and their context. (One page-long note begins "Farting in Afghanistan is far more distressing and shameful than it is in the West." Another is just one line: "In Pashto, diabetes is called 'sugar'.") This might seem unremarkable, but in fact represents a notable intervention on the part of the translator, as clarifications of this kind are most often contained in the introduction or endnotes, or else in an appended glossary. Another bold choice is the inclusion of Seamus Murphy's exceptional photographs, which render the landays 3D. (Some of the photos span two pages, and the ones that are confined to just one beg to be blown-up; I can easily see the book being a heavier, glossier, coffee-table style publication, but am glad it isn't.)

The landays are in part a response to restrictive social conditions. Hingeing on sophisticated double entendres and allusions, they are subversive and politically charged, and, collectively, reflective of a range of political and personal outlooks. Some of the copy I found about the book online compared the poems to tweets, a reference that felt to me, at first, a little disingenuous. But although this comparison turns out not to be such a stretch, the landays are simply more laconic, more incendiary and more shrewd than most of what you'll find on Twitter (and this from an avid user). This is, of course, at least partially down to Griswold's highly engaging translations – but it's difficult to discern to what degree she has altered the landays for an English-speaking readership, given that she provides only a broad outline of her translation strategy, which began with "word by word" translations into English from the Pashto, followed by collaboration with "a handful of native Pashto speakers" on the final texts.

Searching online for information about Griswold, I came across an event page on the Pulitzer Centre website for "a night of Afghan poetry reading, conversation and a short film screening with journalist Eliza Griswold and photographer Seamus Murphy." Above the event description are grayscale photographs of two white faces. In considering the politics of the book, perhaps this might represent a source of contention: two white Americans in the business of collecting and publishing rare elements of Afghan culture. But this book is clearly not Griswold's saviour fantasy, nor does she present her project as the catalyst for her own personal epiphany. If the book can be said to relate any kind of epiphany, it is one transferable to readers regarding our severely limited perceptions of non-English speaking cultures, and others' inner lives – as ambiguous, perverse and contrived as our own.

Unlike a lot of translation work that we might more readily classify as 'radical', including books like Paul Legault's *The Emily Dickinson Reader*, an English-to-English translation of Emily Dickinson's 1,789 poems, or Anne Carson's exploded view of Latin translation as formed via her grief for her dead brother, *Nox*, Griswold's work in translation is radical because of the measures taken at the point of her sourcing her material. Legault's book has been pulled up for its poor handling of the gender dynamic, and although Anne Carson's strategy is notably radical, her source text, Catullus 101, is well-trodden ground. Translating from what we might call, in terms of its representation in literature, a minor language (female expression) within a hermetic poetic form (the landay) within a language scarcely represented in English-speaking literary culture (Pashto), *I Am the Beggar* should cause us to rethink what might constitute a radical translation. Contravening the dominant vectors of culture, books of this kind should also prompt us to think about who most often gets to have their say and why, about what kind of work is most often brought into English through translation, and how our reading habits should not be passive, but active and politically engaged.

In conversation with Muriel Rukeyser's truism "What would happen if one woman told the truth about her life? The world would split open", the landay translations capture the women in Afghanistan's political and social views, their misandry and desire, and "humanity and dark humour". In illustrating the latter, Griswold, in her introduction, relates one of the first landays she heard, as recited to her by a woman named Gulmakai:

Making love to an old man
is like fucking a shriveled cornstalk black with mold.

I Am the Beggar of the World: Landays from Contemporary Afghanistan *by Eliza Griswold and Seamus Murphy is published by Farrar, Straus and Giroux, $15.*

Seamus Murphy
From *I Am the Beggar of the World: Landays from Contemporary Afghanistan*

Gallery

© Seamus Murphy, 2015

© Seamus Murphy, 2015. *Photographs from* I Am the Beggar of the World:
Landays from Contemporary Afghanistan *by Eliza Griswold
and Seamus Murphy (Farrar, Straus and Giroux, 2014).*

PHILLIS LEVIN

Boy with a Book Bag

Father, forgiue them, for they know not what they doe.
    Luke 23:34

He arrived weeks after school had begun,
A boy with a book bag, his gestures
Sluggish and clumsy, the bag too big
For a child to carry – holding what
We didn't know. And though
By the following morning he was gone
For good, and no one except the teacher
Uttered a word about him thereafter,
Mrs Matarazzo only saying
Victor had been "transferred",
The day he was with us something
Entered the room that wouldn't leave.
The light began to change, as it did
Every fall, but something new
Among us remained.

This was the year the radio blared
A crime I thought I could have done.
I wondered if I had an alibi,
But could think of none since I
Could be everywhere at once, inhabit
Any mind, occupy any pair of shoes.
But there was someone I couldn't be:
Victor, sitting close to me.

I don't remember the face of the girl
Who took me aside one day and said
That I killed Jesus, relaying the news
Matter-of-factly, without prologue

Or proof, the verdict clear.
I wasn't sure what she meant
Exactly, but didn't I already believe
That I was capable of anything,
However terrible or grand,
Invisibility at my command?
If I could be accused of killing Christ
Couldn't I be the person the police
Were in hot pursuit of for robbing
A bank at gunpoint in Paterson?
You may ask how a six-year-old
Imagines such a thing, but why not:
What is holding up a bank
Next to murdering Jesus?

                Whether he appeared
Before those suspicions or later,
Victor's brief life in our class
Unleashed so sudden a force
That the awkward bearing
Of his body, his ridiculously serious
Leather book bag, his bland expression
And the mottled pallor of his skin
Form a picture summoned
By the sound of his perfectly
Old-fashioned, inappropriate name.
But his parents may have christened him
Without knowing he would win
Little more than their love,
His intelligence so limited that a room
Of first-graders learning to spell
Could tell right away he didn't belong.

Who did belong? I certainly stuck out,
A strange bird taller than all
The boys and all the girls, afraid to play
Because I didn't know that play
Was all in play. Ordinarily
I shared a desk with David Unger,
My true partner, the two of us
Pretending we were butchers
Trimming the fat off slabs of meat
We made of clay: dear David,
Who doodled in his copybook blissfully
What turned out to be equations
Of trigonometry, perplexing
Even the librarian with his questions.

On this day we were gathered round
A low Formica table, with Victor
Seated among us: the teacher
Led him over after pronouncing
His name. There must have been
A lull, a few minutes of quiet between
Handing in homework and beginning
Another lesson, when we were left
To ourselves. As if responding to a sign,
One child then another reached
Across to the place on the table
Where Victor's right hand
Was resting, and one by one,
With quick jabs, started pinching him.
He didn't cry out, they didn't stop.
Soon everyone had taken a turn
But me: then I too lifted my hand,
Reaching into the ring, but it
Wouldn't go further, it hovered
Above his, unable

To descend. A sensation arose,
Akin to the pressure created
When trying to bring together
Like magnetic poles.

         Then it was over.
All at once Mrs M. was there,
Standing above us, comprehending
What occurred. Pink blotches
And a trail of crescent moons from
The fingernails of children digging in
Covered the back of his hand.
I recall her silence (no reprimand).

They had watched and waited,
And he had watched and waited, too,
For a moment looking up at me
As if in my eyes he could read
What I would do. But I would be
The one who hesitated,
Mute as my useless hand in the air
Refusing to leave a mark on his skin,
Who would not partake of his flesh
Yet could not prevent the slaughter,
Who must atone for
Doing nothing to save him, saying
Nothing to save him, failing him,
Failing to join the others
In sin (they will be forgiven),
Condemned to an island
Of goodness, thereafter to see
The sad look of surprise in his
Uncurious eyes, his hand a lame
Bloated bird, their hands dipping in
For the kill, mine still among them.

SIMON RICHEY

The Emptiness

When the house was taken down
the air that for so long
had been parcelled into rooms
drifted into the day and was lost there.

There were no windows anymore
for the sunlight to fall through,
or landings to rest on, and it fell now
in long beams on the bare ground.

In time the last of the brick dust
was carried off by the wind
and there was only the emptiness,
something like the emptiness

that the horse-drawn wagons,
laden with new bricks,
with window frames and tiles,
had first pulled up at.

Still Life with Words

There is a room
with only a table and a chair in it
and sometimes

a vase of flowers
that is carried into the room
by no more than these words

and set down on the table,
red flowers and yellow flowers
that brighten the whole poem.

GREG DELANTY

The Hellboxer

The nine bitches have put a match to him.
"We're suckin' diesel now, folks. Look out,"
He cries, recasting himself daily in flame.
Here cometh the *great* work, no doubt,
And he doubts everything – includin'
Doubt. Who cares, especially himself,
As long as words come, and they pour molten
From him, hardening into books on a shelf?
What a conflagration. "This is thirsty work.
A drink, please." No better man to suckle the milk
Of Mother Stereotype. Pop goes another cork.
Who's he chatting up now? Typical of his ilk.
This re-newer of the Word, a dismal paradox.
His type cast in the flames of his very own hellbox.

And he thought, way back, he could pull it off
And remain unburnt, unbroken, much to muse ire.
He didn't hear the nine broads, the pyrotechnists laugh:
"Time to turn up the heat, make a human bonfire
Of this devil. Show him who's who. What attitude."
Mind you, they warmed to him when he told
His tearful mother – flaring into a family feud –
He'd be a poet (a corker one at that). Seventeen years old,
And none too bright. She begged him on her knees to
Consider: bank teller, office clerk, any sensible job.
"How'll you make a living? After all we've done for you."
His father looked out of sorts. Flames shot from her gob.
"Besides, you can always write poems in your leisure."
She was just a middle-class dragon minding her treasure.

In the end, he swore, before it was all over,
That he'd call a halt, put his pencil away,
Hang up his cork gun, quietly duck for cover,
Dodge muse abuse. Even the Big G took a day
Off. More than thrice he's heard the cock crow.
Time to reverse, take up the vocation that
As a boy he prayed to have: "When I grow
Up I'd like to be a saint, Lord." He played at
Being humble, pulled off a miracle or two,
Blessed the wicked and poor, renounced desire,
Did penance for the world. Christ, it came true
Perversely, as he hellboxed in the daily pyre
Of being saint and sinner in one. The fire still whips.
He is Jesus planting the betraying kiss on Judas' lips.

[Untitled]

Funny, how with the snaky handle of simply one letter the word
is swiftly unsheathed from its own scabbard, and becomes sword.

JULIAN STANNARD

Émigrés

Now that my neighbours
have returned to Poland

with their gaggle of children
and Mrs Grabowski making

one last indiscriminate visit
to the communal washing-line

I think of sheets, my very own,
hanging somewhere in Gdańsk.

Hermes

Is this your first trip to the Cyclades?
Uncle Billy, he's my second cousin twice removed,
said now that I had some hair above my lip
it was time to visit the land of Petronius
and Aeschylus. Uncle Billy teaches Classics
so he's always coming up with shit like that.
He calls me Hermes, the path-finder, and says
he's going to buy me some golden sandals.

I like it here. Then I ate some toxic octopus:
I was feeling nauseous and slightly psychotic
but in a good kind of way, burning up inside.
Uncle Billy says if you're feeling horny
you need to act on it and the beaches are
driving me nuts. He doesn't mind I'm into girls
and there's this little group of Señoritas
who take almost everything off.

Did I tell you Uncle Billy's paying
for everything, a gift before I take up
post-grad work at UCL? Is UCL any good?
Thanks to the octopus and the Spanish
girls I just couldn't sleep so I asked Uncle Billy
for a Mogadon and he said, Hermes
prepare yourself for the dark side of the moon.
I'm feeling great now. Poetry? I'm mad for it.
Sometimes I lie down with Uncle Billy
and we read poems to each other.
Do you like Rilke? Do you want me to stop?

CAROL RUMENS

Glosa on 'Woman of Spring' by Joan Margarit

Behind words you are all I have.
It's sad never to have lost
a home because of love.
It's sad to die surrounded by respect and reputation.
I believe in what happens in a poem's starry night.

Once, you looked love at me; I saw no hatred.
I must have been the world's worst reader of eyes.
Sorry your nice-girl smiles were mistranslated:
you never would have fobbed me off with lies.
It was the myth I was tending, Heroides,
Harrods, or simply "Let us live..."
Melody of the thousand cadences
Behind words, you are all I have.

When the gods partied, cataracts of fable
poured from your stained pitcher, my statuesque
Iris, a little bruised. Creeps fawned at your table,
warm as the ill-kept wine, and assessed the risk
of an infidelity, shifting shadow by shadow,
and when they heard a fluttering in the grove
of your heavy furniture, they said it's sad
never to have lost a home because of love.

Yellow beacons are feathering the hill,
planned by those same incorrigible suitors.
Your children are dutiful,
quarrying stone, they say, for your new headquarters,
and one day you will ride
out on the shining shoulders of your nation.
If I'm still myself, I'll smirk, make out it's sad
to die surrounded by respect and reputation.

We'll never again meet, and, if we could,
I'd take one look, and make the same mistakes:
panic, nausea, mortification – red
startled to white – the high chant of Sapphics.
Oh, let the apple nod
towards the sunburned hand, bringer of blight.
I myself was once ravished by a god.
I believe in what happens in a poem's starry night.

'Woman of Spring' by the Catalan poet Joan Margarit appears in Tugs in the Fog
(Bloodaxe, 2006), translated by Anna Crowe. The original appeared in Edat Roja, 1991.

Finger Marks

What light is left for us? Not even
the light of that question,
since one of us was nothing light could enter –
a particle of absence in a spectrum
of absences. So, like anyone normal,
we get to caress the intangible,
to name the natures of shadow:
shadow awaited, lovely shade remembered,
shade uncannily clear, shade secretive,
shades massed and breathless
on the snarled terrace, purgatorio of Heysel.

But the shade in the room with us once –
that room with the table, the window, the tree
so many eyes had flown to –
it was caught by the light, and light
found its impersonality,
chè tu se' ombra,
even as I found words – look, I'm still at it –
these wretched smears like the fingers of Statius
on dissolving ankle-bones.

HARRY CLIFTON

Pity and Terror

No, they do not like it. They're afraid –
   The man of foreign extraction
In the second row, and the woman beside him
Out of Ardmore Studios, following the action,
Clutching his elbow. "Die, you shagging bitch,
Or take off back to Crewe across the water –
Do you hear me?" Listening, the daughter
Backs towards the audience, stopping barely an inch

Beyond the double glaze of pity and terror,
   There and not-there.
Again the voice of a mother, through the terrible mirror
Held to themselves. "And what did you ever care
For Irish freedom...? Your father, the IRA."
A trembling hand pours tea, from a real pot,
In mythic space. A distant radio plays.
They're dreaming of the interval, like as not,

That mystery couple. Sure enough, it arrives,
   The space of enlightenment
Everyone here has swung for in a previous life –
The liberal buzz and murmur, Synge's rioters
Gone quiet for an age, between the acts,
In changing motley, waiting. Her and him
The interval bell as certainly drags back
To earlier darkness, as the lights again grow dim

On old age propped on pillows, tea turned gin,
    A table set for one.
Will anything change? Will anyone burst in
From a better world, "Oh Christ, I thought you were gone…",
To work white magic? Lonely on a wall
The lights of a passing car. And time crawls,
The daughter listens again. "That radio,
Turn it off… it was all such a long, long time ago…"

And no, they do not like it. They're afraid,
    Wishing themselves in bed,
Far into each other, a million miles away
On the other side of Abbey Street, Burgh Quay,
Bursting through traffic and rainfall,
Grimed cafés and savage pubs, and the laws
Of iron necessity, to a curtain-call
Beyond Ireland, a freedom without applause.

KATRINA NAOMI

Maybe Owls
for J.S.

The birds in the silver birches listened
as we shone our light over rock
jutting through the moss and grass
of the path. The night silenced us,
we became aware of the still sky
and the stars we were ignorant of.
The need for concentration was there
for the cliff fell away to our left.
At the bend in the path, the birds
took their chance – screeched and flapped
at us, as if we were intruders,
as if we had no right to the dark.
You grasped my arm, my hair,
as you forced my arm over your shoulder
and cowered – an awkward half-kneel,
the torch beam making an involuntary cross
against the woods. I've never known a man
make me hug him. For an instant
I considered if this was all a pretence –
your ornithophobia – but the birds
must have been pleased at their work
for you opened your mouth and screamed,
almost an enjoyment in the pitch of it.
And again – that release.
I used my in-control voice, steady
and slightly stern, which also came
of its own volition. I heard my words,
considered them and our many selves,
considered again the shelter you took
and how the stars didn't recognise us either,
and the night went on, knowingly.

Under my command, we walked back,
faster than we'd come. And you let my arm go.
Stood apart. And I thought, later, maybe owls,
with their whiteness, their bright moon faces,
and how quickly the quiet folded the sounds
away, blending them into the dark, the night
mending itself, the sounds carried
by the river and away down the valley.

Taking Off Billy Collins's Clothes

It will be morning.
I will ask him to place his second cup
of espresso back in its saucer
as quietly as I know he can
and rise from the typewriter.
I will lead him to another window
where it will be snowing –
this and the horses distract him
while I ease off his jacket,
pull his lemon cashmere sweater over his head.
He will scarcely notice while he listens
for the sound snow makes, slipping away
to a reverie of landscapes he's yet to visit.
As I unbutton his jeans,
his coffee breath
blurs the glass momentarily.
I cannot tell you everything
but he kicks away the crumpled denim
as if shrugging off something half-remembered
and I feel that he's stopped himself
from murmuring something wry,
sensing I may prefer silence.

JULIAN TURNER

The Black Box
a brief history of influencing machines

The Original Influencing Machine (1706)
to Francis Hauksbee

I place my hands as gently as I can
around the globe that glows below my skin;
a magic lantern of coronal wind
passes through my skull to touch my mind.
I watch the pictures form out of thin air
as shadows walk and breathe inside the sphere.
I feel the static build as currents swim
and watch my thoughts like dancing cherubim.

A grating noise: I drag the globe across
the stone floor of my den. Inside the room
its astral light illuminates the chaos
of this cluttered life. Despite the gloom
I see things clearly now: inside the ball,
the room. All life is electrical.

The Air-Loom (1797)

to James Tilly Matthews

    machine v; to contrive, plot (against a person)

A thousand operators come and go
in hugger-mugger to this basement room
and carefully avert their eyes in case
they recognise each other in the gloom,
the intricate machine they stand beside –
all copper tubes and bobbins ringed with brass,
distilling thoughts like thread out of thin air –

an instrument of what will come to pass.
The woven thoughts are fired across the street
and sown in minds as dreams begin their light-
show in the brain, becoming part of what
we think is ours, as close as air at night
creeps to our blood, more intimate than touch.
Although the feather breath that brushes you

with its miasmal stealth is not your breath,
you cannot tell it from yourself and, though
inside you and not of you, you won't know.
Next day you find unfathomable thoughts
tucked like bookmarks in between your own,
surprised at knowing things you were not taught.
I've seen these men as they pursue their ends

with grim intrigue and fear what they believe,
have heard about caprices such as theirs
and watched them warp the world into their weave.
When they are done and all their thoughts reside
in heads that steer the foundering ship of state,
they pack away the hardware, slip outside
onto the street and then evaporate.

The Afterlife of the Air-Loom (1919)
to Viktor Tausk

When it had spun its thoughts and left for dead
the poor man in his cell of abscesses,
the ghost machine evolved, became a box
of tricks, all micro-waves and mobile masts,
a soup of circuitry from which it wove
each of the dreams of Man, the vital parts
a baby body cannot fathom out.

A black Ur-box, it sits now on my desk,
a panel on the front, a toggle, wires
entering a sealed socket at the back.
Thus the mind presents the body: as
a nebula of darkness, infinite
inside but small and definite in size.
It hums the hymn of electricity.

If I contained it in another box
and buried it in darkness down below
and sealed them all inside the deepest mine
I could not stop it uttering its thoughts.
Though blank and dangerous, it condescends
to let the mind envisage it and works
its wonders by itself, for its own ends.

How Operators Make You Do (1958)

to Barbara O'Brien

The box is everything – inside its cool,
jet surface something stirs. My smallest thought
is taken by its wavy lines that wash
into my skull and scoop my brain out:
the myth of perfect, svelte machinery
that fires inside a sealed exterior
and makes of me an oiled, hypnotic slave.

The box is magnet, gun and so much more –
it shoots exploding words into my head
and serves them up on plates as word-salad.
It pulls the sentences out of my mouth
as I speak them. I'm porous. When it pours
I fill with rain and, as the box decides,
I reach my tipping point and rain myself.

Remote Surveillance (2012)

It all comes down to us, eventually:
miasma segues into smog, then Clean
Air Acts and radiation reaches out
its wavelengths for impressionable minds.
Our fear is always on the move, switching
between stations, on the look-out for a signal,
those metal ears that turn as the world turns.

We sit at consoles, monitor the screens,
imagining the masters – sat in gantries
quartering the Earth, the data streams,
the market oscillations – keeping tabs
on everything that moves. Neutrino beams
seek out our drop zones, fumble for a thought
and slip it softly through the letterbox.

A false self camped inside each sleeping brain,
Manchurian candidates who dream of power,
fifth columnists inside a conquered mind,
Helsinki syndrome separatists who plan
for someone else the future of us all;
the dreams we dream in sleep laboratories,
that great suggestions box, the mind of man.

BILLY RAMSELL

The Top 10 Luminous Mushrooms of Cerdanya Forest

10

Pony-browns, double-trunked, are a tonic for shoulder trouble, for all known insidious ailments of the upper back. Chop them roughly where they flourish in their vestibular thickets. No dallying. Sauté them in leaf-light, quick as you can, on a skillet hot as you can make it. Add a fist of parsley, a few barbecued slivers of willow bark.

9

Avoid on pain of banishment candy-kisses. Neither pluck them nor enquire as to the ban on their disturbance. Feel at liberty, however, to relish the concert of their pinkish spines, their pastel antiseptic coral that marks the forest's proper border and beginning.

8

Beware, too, of wren-settles. For the merest tongue-full of their salty chalk will abolish seven memories, scouring them – without vestige or residue – from the hippocampus's kernel, from its most convoluted, intimate folds.

7

Further in seek butter-buds: tender polyps most delectable raw, their flaking flesh best savoured by a palate washed in brandy, best presented in ochre marmalade's southern, sultry ooze.

6

Finch-whistles look proverbial with their white-pocked red berets and are a happy mushroom, a party mushroom. One for a good time, two for a bender. Three to re-experience your favourite sexual encounter. Four and for a fortnight you'll dream only in magenta.

5

The mushrooms known as boar-droppings found their poet in Salvador Espriu who designated them "magnificent and bobble-headed sentries of the forest's deeper zones". No stew in all the annals of Catalunya, he declared, had ever suffered by dint of their inclusion.

4

Mary-shells are delicate sub-aqua-seeming flaps and will soothe most minor complaints of women – cramps, sore feet, distemper – but must be ingested unbeknownst to her.

3

Black-shamrock is much sought after by a younger, more aggressive crowd with their faux-hawks, rags and nipple-rings. They gather in the deep forest clearings. They smoke it and are transported where the sweet wood burns at twilight near the well-head; where the men issue first from the crouched wattle dwellings, in masked single file, garbed as stags and foxes; where the ugliest *marujas* of the village offer kindling; where the girl-child closest to fifteen in age gives the first spark to the beacon.

2

Almond-headed pig-pies: so preposterous a confection, in such revolt against likelihood as to render further counsel academic.

1

A scattered shoal; luminous, ridiculous, their intermittent brilliance snaring the eye, flaring in what you know is more than happenstance, sprig-anemones beckon you deeper. For the forest's dimming, innermost precinct is what their luminescence sells. Switching on then off again in unknowable waves, in cycles of fitful glitter though the undergrowth, those spasmodic candles invite you past briars, past thickening soil-breath, down their tapering, convoluted path as evening comes.

AT A TILT

Hans Magnus Enzensberger, New Selected Poems, *Bloodaxe, £15*
ISBN 9781780372501

reviewed by Jamie McKendrick

. . .

In 'Confession', published in his seventieth year, Hans Magnus Enzensberger admits to a weakness: the stirrings of admiration:

Harder and harder for me
are hatred, envy, contempt,
the youthful feelings.

The poem assembles a team of losers, "almost all" of whom have won his respect, and we are left to guess which one hasn't. They are found at the end "unstoppably / feeling their way and burrowing". These figures include an abstemious eater of eggs, an imprisoned politician, "that wife with her six face-lifts" and "the dosser in his kraal of plastic bags". The final word "*wühlen*" (from the verb 'to burrow') suggests a kind of blind activity on their part, an attempt to make themselves at home in a comfortless zone. His admiration is described as "A habit / sweeter than rage / and more dangerous than smoking." Questions hang in the air. Is the poet abjuring his earlier, adversarial politics and settling into mellow old age? Are those youthful feelings more, or less, dangerous? Is the speaker really boasting of a strength while confessing to a weakness? Is he saying good riddance to youth, or worried that this new tendency may make him less vigilant, thus more susceptible to being hoodwinked? The tone is flat and ambiguous; the list of persons, however, is rapid and sparky, and comes across well in David Constantine's translation.

This *New Selected Poems* is a reprint of the 1994 *Selected Poems* with the addition of *Kiosk*, translated by Michael Hamburger and the poet, *Lighter than Air*, translated by Constantine and *A History of Clouds* translated by Esther Kinsky. In his introduction, also reprinted from the former *Selected*, Hamburger prefers "hard-headed" to aggressive as a description of Enzensberger's tone. There are good reasons for hard-headedness in someone brought up in the Third Reich, who in his youth in Nuremberg had Julius Streicher as a next-door neighbour. Enzensberger is a poet naturally disposed to see mildness as collusive with tyranny, as sheepishly abetting the wolves.

Now eighty-six years old, not only one of Germany's greatest modern poets but Europe's too, he has earned the right to be mellow if he wants to be. He may no longer be the *"zornige junge Mann"* (angry young man) that one critic deemed him, but this poem doesn't quite convince us that he's become quiescent with age. Besides, there has always been a tolerance and warmth behind the cool, abrasive style.

In vain, I have been trying to think of an English-language poet with whom he could usefully be compared. (A friend who knows Enzensberger's poetry well suggested Louis MacNeice for his range and intelligence and *joie de vivre*. But even that inspired suggestion seems slightly astray.) Perhaps in Germany, too, he stands as a solitary eminence. Of course every good poet is *sui generis* but it's something else I'm trying to suggest. In Italy, the slightly older poets with a trace of Brechtian lineage like Franco Fortini (born 1917) and Giovanni Giudici (born 1924) share some of his qualities. Both, like Enzensberger (born 1929), are brilliant essayists, their imaginations at once ethically probing, urbane and internationalist. Elsewhere, at least west of Germany, there's nothing parallel that I can think of. The idea that Italian poets of that generation, he and perhaps other Germans such as the far older Günter Eich and the younger Reiner Kunze, should have much in common is not entirely random. They have all had to dig, or burrow, their way out from under the ruins of fascism: politically, culturally, linguistically; and that entailed a deeper, more extreme distrust of culture than has ever been forced upon British or American poets. The need for "a revaluation of all values" was even greater in Germany than in Italy. None of this can make a poet, but a poet of Enzensberger's gifts can, and does, make something out of it.

We can find any number of British poets distrustful of a compromised language and disaffected in politics, but no one like Paul Celan who has had to re-assemble the language out of fragments. Enzensberger is not as radical and fractured as that, but his poems have a sceptical and anti-lyrical tendency. In his lines, politics, philosophy and science often displace the literary. But all this makes his work sound far grimmer, as well as more professorial, than it is. Though sometimes formidable in intellectual reach and confidence, his poems are vivid in their images, unexpected in their movement, and immediately appealing. I mentioned Eich earlier not because his politics – whatever his post-war declarations – are similar but because the starkness of perhaps his best-known poem 'Inventur' (Inventory), which, in Michael Hofmann's translation, begins "This is my cap, / my coat, / my shaving kit / in the burlap bag", seems to have had a telling impact on early Enzensberger, and can be heard, for example in 'Middle Class Blues':

> The grass grows,
> the social product,
> the fingernail,
> the past.
>
> The streets are empty.
> The deals are closed.
> The sirens are silent.
> All that will pass.

Enzensberger's poem shares Eich's rawness and minimalism, though his imagery is more mobile and vagrant.

His 'Historical Process' from 1964 reads like a parable of the Cold War, the world frozen in an identity-less state of torpor: "The ice-breakers will be here by morning. / Then the trawlers will leave [...] So what. / It doesn't matter about your name." (The German line that corresponds to "A fighter howls across the island" is missing from the text.) The repeated, shrugging phrase "So what", set near the beginning and near the end of the poem, acts as a curious framing device.

One feature that is discernible throughout Enzensberger's long career is an almost architectonic feeling for the structure of a poem. Refrain-like repetitions, motifs set at angles to one another, the lack of adornment – all these create an impression of spatial design. In his subtle poem about immigration 'Old Europe' from *Kiosk*, the first two stanzas end with parenthetical questions, which sets up the expectation that the final stanza will follow suit, but instead the reader is confronted by "the dark-green portal / of the Elephant Inn, built in 1639". The asymmetry leaves the poem at a tilt, as if the ancient inn was another exotic, earlier immigrant facing the Guinean selling "key-ring pendants" and "the old Bosnian woman / stretching her stiff legs". Sometimes an entire poem is composed by ringing the changes on a single word or word stem, as in 'The Force of Habit' where "*Gewohnheit*" (habit) or its cognates appear twenty-two times in thirty-eight lines. This causes understandable obstacles for Hamburger's translation, which must deploy several words for the one German root: "habit" and "habitual" have to give way to "ordinary", "extraordinary", "gets used to", "usual", "are used to": "Ordinary people ordinarily do not care / for ordinary people". The original's elegantly twisted logic and virtuosic wordplay founders in the English, through no real fault of the translator. In another such poem, which the poet himself translates, the name Dante occurs at least once in all but one of its seventeen lines. Opening "This is not Dante", it ends:

> This is a man who believes he is Dante.
> This is a man everybody, except Dante, believes to be Dante. [...]
> This is a man nobody believes to be Dante, except Dante.
> This is Dante.
>
> ('Identity Check')

It's a kind of 'House that Jack Built', enacting a dizzying identity crisis that might be taking place at a border crossing or a police station. The title of this poem in German is a gobstopper of bureaucratese: '*Erkennungsdienstliche Behandlung*'. The literal meaning of the phrase is 'official recognition treatment', basically identification via photo and fingerprinting. Enzensberger renders it as 'Identity Check', which suffers a considerable loss of syllables. Like the Marxian 'Historical Process', his titles abound in idiolects, dehumanising jargon, philosophical flotsam:

'Model Towards a Theory of Cognition', 'Delete the Inapplicable', 'A Hare in the Data Processing Centre'. His poems have an insatiable appetite for language, and in the final poem of this selection, 'A History of Clouds', even include the mathematical formula of Kepler's Conjecture regarding the stacking of spheres: where the scientist "saw the atomic grid, guessed / its rotational symmetry, / sixty degrees, calculated / its packing density: $\pi/2\sqrt{3}$". This is way above my head, but I suppose for those, like Enzensberger, who can follow the thought (he has written a delightful book for children about numbers), these abstract symbols are a kind of poetry. More approachable and of wider appeal is his 'Ode to Stupidity':

> how you shine from the bloodshot eyes of the hooligan
> and trip along in upper-class arrogance clearing its throat,
>
> and how you waft at us with a bedraggled Muse's bad breath
> and as polysyllabic delirium in the philosophy seminar.

Even here, where you expect a Popean "universal Darkness" to descend, the poem unpredictably changes tack at the end, offering a merciful reprieve: "only to the elect do you grant the rarest of your gifts, / the blessed simplicity of the simple."

The introduction refers to Enzensberger's *Mausoleum* (1975) as a "book of prose poems". This is misleading: that collection does include some prose poems but is mainly of verse, and it is one of Enzensberger's most original works. It would have been worth including something from Joachim Neugroschel's translation, now out of print, but the *New Selected* is already a hefty four hundred pages. Hamburger's translations are themselves hard-headed, versatile and ably play the idiomatic against the conceptual, but still it's a relief to come to Enzensberger's own translation of *The Sinking of the Titanic* – though it's vexing he should also be such an accomplished *English* poet. He's the exception to the rule that you can only be a poet in your mother-tongue. These lines from 'Apocalypse. Umbrian Master, about 1490', one of many poems to explore the pictorial, may serve as an example:

> Destroying the world is a difficult exercise.
> Hardest to paint are the sounds – for example
> the temple veil being rent asunder, the beasts

roaring and the thunderclaps, Everything, you see,
is to be rent asunder and torn to pieces,
except the canvas.

There's nothing showy about the writing, but the rhythmic variety, from the dactylics of the second line to the iambics and trochaics of the third, and the gradual pace and economy of detail are all effective. It gives the reader none of the unease that poetry in translation can sometimes induce, that feeling that the essential thing is "subject to loss by evaporation", as packets of tobacco used to warn before they were emblazoned with scarier stuff. If, as Enzensberger says, admiration is "more dangerous than smoking", this book should carry a health warning.

Jamie McKendrick's Out There *(2012) is published by Faber.*

SINGING THE BODY ELECTRIC

Greta Stoddart, Alive Alive O, *Bloodaxe, £9.95*
ISBN 9781780371511
Matthew Siegel, Blood Work, *CB editions, £8.99*
ISBN 9780909585058

reviewed by Carol Rumens

. . .

Two collections, profoundly concerned with mortality, proclaim its opposite in their titles. Greta Stoddart's *Alive Alive O* (after the apocryphal Dublin fishmonger's famous street-cry) strikes an informally defiant note – a spirit echoed by the energy and physicality of the poems. Siegel's quieter acknowledgement of the mechanics and maintenance involved in staying healthily alive-alive-o, *Blood Work* alludes to his treatment for Crohn's disease, and, perhaps, to writing the narrative of that struggle. His collection is a guide to the arts of living with personal illness, Stoddart's, a guide to the arts of mourning and redeeming personal loss. Passionately attuned to the individual, both address the universal hunger to challenge biblical and biological truism: in the midst of death, they remind us, we are in life.

Stoddart's work is widely acclaimed and needs little introduction to readers. Her third collection, nevertheless, represents an advance. Colloquial, faintly unruly, the poems travel light on adventures of consciousness, channelling the energies of a big, agnostic imagination into new forms. There's nothing lapidary about Stoddart's recent work: even her meditations engage with physical movement. In the collection's opening poem, for instance, "the curtain" is only partly funereal, and comes with associations of theatrical business, and even a whiff of adrenaline:

> No tears then. Just one of us to hold
> aside the curtain – *here we are, there you go* –
> before letting it slump majestically back
>
> to that oddly satisfying inch above the boards
> in which we glimpse a shadowy shuffling dark.
>
> ('The Curtain')

Stoddart's para-theology dares to be un-consoling. The unique and personable ghosts of 'Stars' are nonetheless annoyingly unresponsive and unassimilable: "They can't even move. / They're just there, burning up the past." In 'ICU', a narrative woven from the vigorous practical activities and painful conversations of intensive care, all the movement jolts to a halt in the last quatrain, a brutally unembellished cul-de-sac of not-seeing-you, underlined by insistent repetitions:

> Where is your husband now, where your father?
> In a dark room that had to be left.
> We had to leave it. We had to leave
> That dead face to its dead self.

The conflict of movement and stasis is differently dramatised in the three-poem sequence, 'House and Train'. In the first poem, the speaker, on the train, passes her own house, marvelling that it can keep all its events and secrets inside "without / a single alteration to its footings". The second depicts, in unpunctuated blocks of print, the four windows of that house, finding for each a characteristic exchange of inside/outside energies ("This is the one you close you / say to keep out the cold but / really it's that bird you want / to stop..."). In the third poem, the speaker is inside the house looking out at the train where, framed in one of its windows, a figure, presumably herself, is so completely absorbed in movement that "nothing will stay still long enough to hurt her". Different writers employ different tempi, reflecting the rhythms of their own blood-work. For Stoddart, the pace is brisk, and her house and train ultimately merge metaphors, forming a space-time continuum, a flux of interchange.

Every poem is different, the claustrophobia of line and form differently challenged. There is physical mimesis, with shaped poems like 'Wild Pear' or the stepped caesuras of 'Turning Earth'. Other poems draw on the rhythms of traditional verse, not only to utter lamentation but to summon a *Walpurgisnacht* of whirling, restless spirits ('All those turning') or, in the seamless collage of invention and quotation that is 'Letter from Sido', ventriloquise the plaintive and sharply frank epistle of a dying mother to her daughter:

> I can hear my pen scratching in the dark.
> I have grown very thin.
> When I'm at the water pump in the morning
> I feel my dress touch the backs of my legs,
> the sun is just warm and I feel ten years old.
> How can I leave now?

"What's out that's not in?" asks the speaker in Stoddart's prose-poem 'Interior', a painfully important question for the less metaphysically orientated poet of *Blood Work*. Matthew Siegel, born in New York in 1984, makes a poised and engaging debut with this collection. The brief epigraph from Walt Whitman's *Song of Myself* ("You my rich blood!") alerts us to a significant influence. Siegel is homey and intimate, not a free-wheeler of the open road (if any contemporary poet could be) but, in a more attenuated, delicate form, that generous admission of physicality, that particular treasuring of the human, pervade his work. In fact, Whitman's loaded question "And if the body were not the soul, what is the soul?" lies at the heart of many of the poems in both these new collections.

Blood's job is to keep the embodied soul together, and the haemorrhage of "the bright red life" beyond its confines, for Siegel as for John Keats, is ominous and shocking. The terror is never quite forgotten, and the last poem in the book returns to it. But bloodshed is also part of the voluntary and happier processes of treatment. Siegel takes the reader by the hand, as if promising, initially, at least, not to scare us: he even has a fox visiting "the fox hospital" in the first poem, and almost evades whimsy by noting the literary strategy.

Throughout the collection, the poetic surface is smooth, rhythmically and tonally, as if language itself were a container that had to be held steady. Evenly paced couplets in the title poem mime a professionalism that's reassuring but faintly suspect ("the woman who draws from me smiles, always / remembers me, no matter how skinny I get") before it delves under the pleasantries for a darker image of unequal power-relations:

> [...] I don't tell her
> the best to take my blood was a different woman
>
> who used to draw blood from animals,
> part the fur, find their blue tap and drain.

And still, at the end of the poem, when the gently infantilised patient is allowed to "play with" the warm, blood-filled tubes, he thinks subversively of "condoms, tissues / all the things that contain us but cannot."

Siegel challenges continence on metaphorical rather than formal levels. A favourite image first appears when, in the Whitman-interrogative sequence, 'The electric body', the speaker remembers visiting Dr Chen in California: "At the bottom of his clear mug, / a bag of green tea bled into hot water". Opposing the need to contain and control there is always the longing to release and "expel". Sleeping in a bed that's too small for his adult size, the speaker retrieves the oozing terror of the metaphor when the ceiling's "giant hand" presses "his entire body like a teabag in hot water".

Blood Work has five sections, interlinked but differentiated through shifts between self and others, private and public ownership of the body. The poems in III, addressed to Mother, movingly respond to a woman *in extremis* among the domestic banalities, someone both intimately known and a stranger: "Tiny black bits float in the water pitcher / and I think *how does she live this way?*" ('Soap'). A scattering of ekphrastic poems gives Siegel further purchase on the strange or surreal, but, in the photographs he imagines for us, the bodies are never stilled, never denied personality. *Blood Work* is grounded, even sensible, the self-deprecation apparent in the habit of using chattily confessional titles, placed in parenthesis and repeated in the first line: '(My pills doze until I wake them)', '(Mother puts on my lipstick)', '(It's true what you've heard about my mouth)'. In the latter poem, the lonely, hungry body literally becomes electric, and the shadow of history casts a sardonic chill:

> It's true what you've heard about my mouth.
> Radio signals in the fillings, sparks in the snap
> of mints in the dark. I am silent and afraid
> and I find comfort in world news watching
> everything blow up except my apartment.
> I'm aware this is very American of me.

Long may this poet's quiet but resonant signals keep coming.

Carol Rumens's next collection, provisionally titled Animal People, is due from Seren in 2016.

HAPPY VALLEY

Jack Underwood, Happiness, *Faber, £10.99*
ISBN 9780571313617
Sarah Howe, Loop of Jade, *Chatto & Windus, £10*
ISBN 9780701188696

reviewed by William Wootten

. . .

The promise of Sarah Howe and Jack Underwood has already been spotted and rewarded. The names of their mentors, editors, poetry groups, universities and awards are to be found in the acknowledgements pages of these, their first full collections. So, with both poets already in their early thirties, and with their books each bearing the stamp of a commercial press, one now hopes to find, not just signs of their promise, but evidence of their achievement.

Underwood, who has a PhD in Creative Writing, a subject he now lectures in, is certainly a sparky performer. His deployment of varying types of blank verse can be pleasingly deft; he can have an attractively expansive tone of poetic address; he is also quite a phrasemaker. Metaphors and similes may be just the smart side of cliché: "The streets look like they want to be frying eggs / on themselves" or grand and luxurious (though, in this case, unlikely to float): "Sometimes your sadness is a yacht // huge, white and expensive, like an anvil / dropped from heaven". Mild surprises

in diction, or in the succession of sentences, have a quirky zip: "Spring //
is here so now the plants and animals / are starting to have sex again.
We've unblocked / the drain of its crud and bumf; the smell is waning."

Still, a successful poem is more than a series of attention-grabbing
tones and phrases. And here Underwood can run into trouble. 'Inventory
of Friends' begins: "I run through the grass-topped lives of my friends", a
line at once celebratory yet bringing to mind the grass of the graveyard. But
the poem fails to live up to its opening, and by the time we get to "I try to
imagine having / her mind: funny, smart and odd as twenty / emperor
penguins filing through the door / of a black limousine", the would-be
arresting lines have become merely flashily diverting, the poem's potential
squandered.

Underwood has a fondness for hypothetical subject matter: what if "I
lived in a cave and you were my only visitor"; what "If guns // were more
popular in our culture"? What if I injected blood into a banana in order
to see how people would respond? What if I had a child and failed to look
after it? What if I'd had a sister who'd died and believed myself haunted
by her ghost? In these last two cases, some of the details are undoubtedly
well drawn. Yet since, according to the poems, Underwood hasn't yet got
a child, and, it turns out, never had a sister either, they still feel contrived
and manipulative. More generally, the poems in *Happiness* tend to read
as if occasioned, not by pressure of life or the imagination, but by casting
around for a subject for a poem, the aping of first-hand experience and
the desire to get a response. It's only when the subject genuinely seems to
disturb Underwood himself, as it does in the 'The Ashes' and 'Wilderbeast',
in which death and the sexual devil become not just scary masks but
entities capable of grabbing both poet and reader, that he actually achieves
the reaction he so often seeks to force.

Underwood's poetic influences are well assimilated, though largely
restricted to recent mainstream British poets and the odd contemporary
American. And when his poetry does make use of the poetry of the more
distant past – as when he riffs on John Donne's 'The Good Morrow' by
asking "Were we gherkins bobbing / in our harmless jars"? – the result
could scarcely be labelled a profound communion. Sarah Howe's poetic
influences spread deeper and wider; her overt encounters with poets past
and present are less bumptious. Occasionally, she writes apprentice *homage*
('The Countess of Pembroke's Arcadia' is wannabe Geoffrey Hill;
'MONOPOLY (*after Ashbery*)' is as advertised) or an ill-fated exercise in

style ('Start with Weather'). But the way Howe has schooled herself in the work of a host of twentieth-century British and, more especially, American poets results in considerable stylistic range: along with the loose-ish blank verse there is free verse, a host of stanza shapes, as well as some very convincing prose poetry. Moreover, Howe, who teaches Renaissance English literature, also possesses an impressive knowledge of earlier English, Chinese, Greek and Roman literature and culture.

Howe has the rare ability to write poems that clearly relate to the academic study of literature yet which are not, in the bad sense, academic. 'Sirens' is, in essence, an essay on Theodore Roethke's 'Elegy for Jane'. It is artful, insightful and unpretentiously erudite in the way it uses fascination with Jane's "pickerel smile" to explore both Roethke's themes and images and wider mythological female figures and themes of doubleness. But what makes the poem is its ability to feel its way into Roethke's lines, their characters and their relationship. This quality of empathic reimagining is one of Howe's greatest assets. Whether she is revisiting her mother's tales of childhood or relating the imprisonment of Ezra Pound, she manages both to treat her protagonists sensitively and to be a live presence on the margins of their stories, making second-hand subject matter appear not stale and appropriated but fresh and shared.

Howe, who has a Chinese mother and an English father, was born in Hong Kong and moved to England as a child. This dual identity and inheritance gives her a favoured theme, though one whose treatment always comes across as personal, felt and particular, not programmatic. It also bequeaths her source materials and subject matters we're unused to in English poetry. And while I'm sure both will seem far less novel to Chinese eyes than to mine, having witnessed Howe's ability to give oft-rehearsed Western tales worthwhile revisits I would be surprised if familiarity would much diminish one's respect for the ways in which they are employed. The poems on Chinese subjects do, however, tend to heighten the sense of wonder and the sensuous evocation. Occasionally, this strays into straightforward overwriting – a slight problem with 'Crossing from Guangdong' – but the richness of texture can be appropriate, as well as beautiful, tallying especially well with the child's-eye view, as is the case with the fine sequential poem 'Islands'. Nor does it preclude the examination of more troubling parts of Howe's Chinese inheritance – the "tale of the woodsman's daughter. Born with a box / of ashes set beside the bed" is no less an examination of the low status of women and the infanticide of girls by its being related in the magical terms of the folk tale. The treatment of what Howe's note cautiously refers to as the "Tiananmen incident" in '*Innumerable*' gains, not lessens, in strength by keeping to her own recollections of that day as a five-year-old at the "Jockey Club's Happy Valley track".

Such restraint in the face of such subject matter is at the opposite pole from that sensationalism without substance one can find in Underwood. Indeed, it is one of a number of qualities and excellences which make the majority of poems in *Loop of Jade* not just promising – as the poems in Underwood's *Happiness*, for all my reservations, undoubtedly are – but mature and accomplished. *Loop of Jade* is one of the best first collections I've read in recent years.

William Wootten's The Alvarez Generation *(2015) is published by Liverpool University Press.*

CURIOUSER AND CURIOUSER

Christopher Reid, The Curiosities, *Faber, £14.99*
ISBN 9780571321452
Caitríona O'Reilly, Geis, *Bloodaxe, £9.95*
ISBN 9781780371467

reviewed by Eamon Grennan

. . .

The opening poem of Christopher Reid's new collection reveals some of his most striking and entertaining qualities: immediacy of address coupled with a strong speaking voice; a sense of performance and persona; an attitude that's part detached comedy, part the wink and nod of knowingness, part genial companionability. The voice in 'The Clowns' is that of a humorous, plain-speaking, politically alert observer ("His courtiers are no help – he hasn't any; / ditto, the palace guard"). Speedily colloquial, this mix of humour and political scepticism defines a particular point of view – one, however, that doesn't tempt us to identify it with the poet himself, instead locating it decisively in this invented character. So, no surprise that 'The Clowns' should concern a king who puts on, or has put on him, motley. Put-on indeed. In this motley compendium of "curiosities" – each poem a bravura description of a particular object, animal, situation, event, whatever (and each title a definite article and substantive noun beginning with the letter C) – motley's your only wear.

What I love in Reid's work is the sheer brio with which each poem is carried off. No subject seems alien to this shrewd, sharp, but often also deeply sympathetic observer of the human condition – especially there where men and women most complicatedly interact. For a great many of these seventy-three poems explore variations on the theme of sex – from genuine affection through machismo, feminisma, pornography, socio-sexual mores and morals, love, loss, and so on. Often throughout such poems, as with others, there's a curiously mixed point of view that can swivel between detachment and compassion. But this is a poet who, no matter the angle of his gaze, is always a genial, urbane, informed, inventive, emotionally astute companion.

His voices are many – from cynic sensualist to the pedantic exactitude of the post-modern scholar who will (in 'The Chocolate') "propose to articulate / a comprehensive erotics of chocolate." Here, as in other poems, Reid's control of a particular idiom, its jargon, is expert and happily entertaining. And the "erotics of chocolate" are just that, bringing things to their proper climax and jouissance with his final lines: "let me pop a square... / on to your moist and acquiescent tongue".

Reid stands in the very English line of wit, civility, epigram and surprise. A poem like 'The Calm', for example, reads like a little fragment of Donne: witty, exact, active and contemplative, lodged in quickened common speech, and startling us by a sudden opening lunge into direct address:

> Becalmed, we had little to do
> but watch ice grow.
> It crept and clenched to form,
> horizon-wide, a lid
> beneath which whales, our old
> companionable foe,
> wantonly hid.

Or in 'The Calabash' you'll hear a Herbert brought cheekily up to date: "Having fashioned the first man out of sticks and mud, / God looked at him and thought, 'Not bad.' But Man / was of a different opinion."

One of the things I like most about these poems is their genuinely relaxed manner of address. "Being dead, I was ready for / the journey" is how 'The Coin' begins, while 'The Concept' opens thus: "Here's my idea: I'll ransack / your wardrobe and drawers / for the naughtiest bits and pieces / I can find to put on". What's impressive is the ease of the conversational, no matter the outlandishly *outré* nature of the content: the poet is always amiably there beside you: confiding in you, surprising and enlightening you.

An important element in this dazzlingly various collection (hard to find another book of poems containing so many riffs on so many diverse subjects: crossroads, canoodling, cufflinks, corncrakes, cheating, and eight-and-sixty more) is the number of translations or "versions" it contains. Mostly (and, to some tastes, with varying success) Reid renders his originals into his own laid-back colloquial style. So here's a Petrarch crossed with Catullus, a Theocritus in cowboy slang, a scabrous Welsh medieval tale, a lovely piece of Sappho, and successful encounters with Apollinaire, Cavafy and others. Likewise this compendious collection includes Reid's versions of fragments of myth (Actaeon, Ariadne, Orpheus et al). His method, again grounding them in ordinary language, normalises them to good, usually comic effect and brings them over – like translations – into a carefully calibrated commonplace version of themselves.

I think of Reid's book as a many-sectioned praise-song celebrating that essential element of his imagination: its curiosity, a condition of perpetual investigative surprise, and the ability to give his surprise and curiosity such embodiment in language that we learn to be more curious and more vigilant ourselves to the brave new worlds always under our gaze. 'The Corbel', for example, is described as "these sports of the mason's fancy – / sandstone doodles, curiosities, jokes", turning them to an art that is at once casual, pointed, humorous, and enduring. Objects, that is, like his own poems that sometimes "cock their snook / at reason and decorum."

The imagination and poetic intelligence behind Caitríona O'Reilly's brilliant third collection operate in a very different way from Reid's. While her opening poem, 'Ovum', is a tour de force of etymological play that might remind us of how Reid can enter and spin a subject, catching its curiosity from many surprising angles, the burden of O'Reilly's poem is more emotionally edgy, seems always at some mostly unspoken risk, and is in the end sadder than Reid's voice-making, his serious ludic performance. His playful "erotics of chocolate" finds another slant in 'Ovum': "It's like putting your mouth to the smooth / breast of the ocarina, from oca, the goose, / hooting out its fledgling notes."

If it is an English tradition of epigram, wit and common sense that lies behind Reid, it is Muldoon who stands (at some distance) behind this particular O'Reilly poem. Transformative as her poems can be, their imaginative commitment is not to his essentially comic angle on or view of the world. It is some sense of reined-in self-exposure that drives her best poems into a kind of intensity that is never part of Reid's intention. In subject, voice, attitude and persona, Reid ranges over a wide world of curiosities, while O'Reilly plumbs her own single and singular, obliquely observed psychic and emotional depths.

As well as confronting what appears to be illness (see especially her title poem, 'Geis', an Irish word meaning oath, taboo, curse, gift) there's an erotic core to her work – eros tangled by its attendant infinite qualifications. A plangent lyricism drives an implicit narrative of emotional complexity, a narrative carried along on wave after wave of hyper-tense, lyrically charged language that could at times owe something to Medbh McGuckian: "My chief want: / the gold-and-olive chasing of your glance, / a look of nakedness and clear fathoms" ('Hunger'). Her poems act as pick-locks in situations that are often presented in terms of imprisonment – everywhere there are captives, prisons, enclosures, dead ends evaded. Sometimes she employs a freshly articulated myth as narrative frame, as in 'Ariadne': "There's a smell // of sex and sulphur – / the atmosphere / of rutting's recent." Even the rhythms can have their own jumpy motion and logic. "And I was a bird", she says in the title poem, "hedge-snared / on a trunk of writhing stone, / nervous with looking through desire's dry cage." In the stillness of the watchful, ever-active mind, she registers the kinetic urgencies of desire and unsparing self-knowledge, her aim being to utter "all the stuttering truths the throat can hold".

The poems in *Geis* often enact a contest between speech and silence. "What is it to talk about silence?" she asks in 'Snow', spotlighting a preoccupying problem, the one she returns to, implicitly or explicitly, in so much of the work. "Are there words for what I felt / in the faceted garden?" she asks, realising that snow is "a vast multitudinous silence" that gives her relief, a relief partly embodied by her rhetoric itself (note the breathy Latinate enlargement of that "multitudinous"). No surprise, then, to find a reference in 'Autonomy' to "tongue-cut women". And given the febrile yet sensuous intensity of her language, her best poems can never be reduced to paraphrase. They are fully alive in their own unfolding

– image by image, feeling by complicated feeling, like the Japanese word *komorebi* for a particular manifestation of light through leaves, but for which, she says, there is "no exact English translation".

"For years I have sought to know", she says in 'Autonomy', and it could be the mantra of many of the best pieces here. Her search for knowledge – at once philosophically focused, and enraptured by all kinds of unlikely data – is conducted in a language bristling with illuminations: "The wound of the mouth closes / ... a radiant stone is placed on the tongue", yet it always moves with careful grace, its own well-laden, fluent momentum. There's even something Keatsian in her assertion, "It is our calling to be lost in detail", as she ranges – wide-eyed, taking all in – among curiosities: airships, Pleistocene snail, wolf spider, "the nipples of the pelargonium". After O'Reilly's impressive earlier volumes in 2001 and 2006, this much-anticipated third collection shows a poet of achieved voice writing at the confident top of her own bent.

Eamon Grennan's There Now *is published by Gallery.* Out of Sight: New & Selected Poems *appeared from Graywolf in 2010.*

ENDGAMES

Mark Doty, Deep Lane, *Cape, £10*
ISBN 9780224099837
Tom Sleigh, Station Zed, *Graywolf, £11.99*
ISBN 9781555976989

reviewed by Conor O'Callaghan

. . .

Endings are important. Here's John Donne on them: "The whole frame of the poem is a beating out of a piece of gold, but the last clause is the impression of the stamp, and that is it that makes it current." They don't sermonise like that anymore!

We should distinguish between the end of the poem and a poem's ending. The former is a long-haul schema to which each fresh essay provides partial means. The latter is the moment when that beating stops; when words suddenly drop off a cliff-edge into darkness; when the poem's given form, in Yeats's memorable coinage, "comes right with a click like a closing box".

If Yeats was right, if the hearing of the "click" when the poem shuts itself complete is the truest version of inspiration, then Mark Doty's gift has perhaps always been questionable. There is no doubting Doty's 'importance' as chronicler of the AIDS epidemic and its aftermath. There is equally no doubting that his poetry has always possessed a clear end in this respect: when we read a Doty poem, we know where the thing is inevitably headed as part of a whole project. But the poems themselves very often struggle to end. Having started as a page-and-a-halfer of the American mode, these days he drags across acres of paper with little discernible exit strategy. The last poem of *My Alexandria*, his most celebrated collection, asks:

> Who can become lost in a narrative,
>   if all he can think of is the end?
>
>   ('Lament-Heaven')

Meaning life and death, yes, but surely aesthetics also. Maybe Doty has no investment in the endings of poems which otherwise succeed, repeatedly, in becoming lost in their own narratives.

Doty's ninth outing, *Deep Lane*, is a deeply nostalgic collection. It is nostalgic for the intensity of youth and desire; for anger and suffering; even for meaning. The material now feels very familiar. Lots of dogs, tattoos, self-harm and experiments with narcotics. Lots of ghosts, be they parents come back to console or dead friends or old flames. Lots of echoes of Whitman and Bishop and a plethora of other scribblers and dribblers. Lots of versions of that symbolic livestock which has conveniently crossed the paths of Yankee poets in recent generations. Lots of desire and beauty. Lots of the unknowable and the unsayable, for heaven's sake.

Doty's quest for transcendence in the face of mortality's inevitable horror generates passages of beautiful writing. His delectation of the material of language remains enviably carnal. The staggered sequence of title poems, for example, recreates the erotic in gardening:

> Dusky skin of the tuber, naked worms
> who write on the soil every letter,
> my companion blind, all day we go digging,
>
> harrowing, rooting deep. Spade-plunge
> and trowel, sweet turned-down gas flame
> slow-charring carbon [...]

The trip at the core of 'Crystal' is positively visionary:

> I went riding all night on Tear Me Apart Road,
> midnight all night, slick gates smashed by storm cloud,
> the hour one roaring bell, and I could live inside

that never-ceasing, further, long after
I thought there was anything more to let go, I
let go the reins and the wheel [...]

Alas, such pluses are fleeting. Doty is simply no nature poet. He cannot see the detail in front of him without trying to impose symbolism on it. One poem, 'What is the Grass?', muses upon a student's bemused marginalia which questions Whitman's famous question with her own: *"Isn't it grass?"* Funny, and yet the wit and profundity of both questions back-to-back get drowned in Doty's subsequent signature whiny cerebration:

And while first I imagine her the very type
of the incurious, revealing the difference
between a mind at rest and one that cannot,

later I come to imagine that she
had faith in language

And while first I imagine? Please. Things as they are serve only as occasions for Doty's analysis of them and of the terms he chooses for his analysis. With a tediousness that is breathtaking, successive poems interrupt themselves to tease out rhetorically (and frequently parenthetically) the *mot juste*:

and in the gathering twilight (what is it that is gathered,
who is doing the harvesting?)

('Deep Lane')

Then he entered me, so to speak,

though I knew I was the one walking
without hesitation through the door he held open,
and *in a moment* I want to write I did cough

but that is suddenly the crux of it:
moment, what is that?

('Crystal')

(I want to spell *long*

with two n's, as Milton spelled
dim with a double m
to intensify the gloom of hell)

('Underworld')

There is not a single poem collected here that does not whiff of the grad seminar room, where Prof Doty pauses proceedings to drift down yet another self-tickled semantic scenic route. Add to that the permission he grants himself to sprinkle his lines with abstractions. Simply saying *awe* and *immanence* ad nauseam does not create any clearer feel for the awesome or the immanent. Simply alluding to illustrious antecedents at every available juncture does not make you of their company.

Then there is the issue of the endings. Poems meander on far too long, apparently for no good reason other than they have no idea how to stop. Some end on rhetorical questions, which always feels like an unsatisfactory cop-out and not really an ending. Instead, they engage in a simulacrum of intensity that feels as weary as it is wearying. When he describes how another poet "writes now / some puffed-up simulation / – a sentimental elegy", an implicit self-critique seems possible.

All of these elements come together in the three-and-a-half pages of 'This Your Home Now', about a seat in a barber shop that leads to the deep lane of memory's dead souls. Etcetera. On it rambles, with a dull genial confessionalism that masks a real anxiety about its ending. The ending, when it comes, responds to an aside on the poem's first page where the poem is paused by parentheses to remark that a friend of Doty called Marie (Howe?) says that all his poems have a *then* in them and he argues that it is the *then* that makes it a poem. The ending, unpunctuated, goes:

I'm going down to Jane Street, to a coffee shop I like,
and then I'm going to write this poem. Then

A breezy gesture of faith in the future? Or plain lame? The latter, I fancy. Lots of gold in the forms of intelligence and nice writing. But that ultimate absence of any conclusive stamp renders poem after poem counterfeit and devoid of any real currency.

The poetry of Tom Sleigh enjoys little of the adulation afforded to Mark

Doty's. He has nothing of Doty's surface 'importance'. Or putting it another way, the white, middle-class, middle-aged heterosexual male author of eight elegant collections has no obvious critical constituency. However, one might reasonably argue that Sleigh is a finer poet than Doty and one worthy of a bigger reputation.

The end suggested in the title of his new collection, *Station Zed*, is not merely alphabetical. As one of the best poems in the book explains, the term comes from the concentration camps, it "turns out to be an SS joke – you came in at Gate A / and went out at Station Zed". The constituency Sleigh's work assumes, then, is the most obvious one: our world and its ongoing history of wars and suffering. More particularly, it is about how the white, middle-class, middle-aged male finds it "hard to know what tone to take when the truth is both atrocious and banal".

Station Zed is broken into four distinct sections, the first and last of which are made up of assorted lyrics. There is, for example, a gorgeous address to a stepdaughter. One sequence recalls the atmospheric Cold War gloom of the poet's youth. The opening poem riffs on the 'Ballad of Mary Hamilton', overlaying images of the original folk song and the poet on the road in contemporary America, and ending:

> Last night there were four Toms,
>   today they'll be but three:
> there was Tom Fool, Sweet Tooth Tom,
>   Tom the Bomb, and me.
>   ('Homage to Mary Hamilton')

Sleigh ends brilliantly: time and again, his forms and their exquisitely minted imagery exit together, they vanish into darkness hand-in-hand at the perfect moment. His handling of form is mostly faultless, too. Sonnets, sestinas, prose poems, a species of loose terza rima, free verse: he seems equally at ease in all of these. Added to that is the distinct impression that here is a poet intent on shaking off the tag of being merely intelligent and elegant. There is a free-and-loose capaciousness to this new work that feels fresh and true. Even when the material is decidedly dark, Sleigh is delighting in the voluble language he has found for it:

> So come on, to hell with it, let's go eat weeds,
> eat the flesh and fruit of our stupid

tears and moans, of our pickled melancholy souls.

Come on! Let's go! So what if I'm wounded – let's go
drink what's already been drunk,
let's go, crow, and find another crow to fuck.

('Homage to Vallejo')

The middle two sections concern Sleigh's experience as a journalist in North Africa and the Middle East. The stand-alone section about Iraq, 'Homage to ', is arguably the highlight of the collection and a remarkable achievement in its own right. It takes the form of *The Narrow Road to the Deep North*, in that a plain prose narrative (the Tigris and Euphrates seen from helicopter or plane, memories of conversations with students) and lyric interludes (a double villanelle, a translation from an original Sumerian fragment) weave in and out of one another. What makes the work remarkable is the complete absence of any judgement in the tone, just a desire to locate a truth beyond the merely factual. There is one especially moving story in which a young woman reads aloud her memory of her brother kissing her goodbye before heading out to suicide-bomb a market, and to which the haunted poet understandably keeps returning. There is an astonishing sestina about routine brutality towards detainees, 'Deposition', employing vacuous military jargon to render the form's refrains almost invisible.

On the downside, to be fair, Tom Sleigh is a bit of a page-and-a-halfer himself. There is something about American poets' innate horror of white space on the page. This is a decidedly chunky, garrulous book, running to over one hundred pages, and very few of those pages are not crammed with big long lines. In spite of his fine sense of form, too many of the stanzas fall too routinely into single sentence units. Some of the lines are so long as to lose any audible natural rhythm: "As if he were a solid melting to liquid turning to gas feeding a flame." Perhaps surprisingly for a poet who invokes Matsuo Bashō, there is almost zilch here resembling miniaturist delicacy. There is the recurring worry that poems are being prompted by reading rather than experience ("I read a story...", "I read once that..."), so that the impetus can come over as second-hand and lacking visceral immediacy. And like Doty, he is not shy of invoking those poets in whose tradition he wishes to be included: Homer, Bashō , Vallejo, Tranströmer... We all do it. But some overdo it, as if blagging their way into a particular room, flattering themselves by insisting on belonging.

However, such shortcomings detract little from the achievement of *Station Zed*. As if conscious of them, the collection ends by meditating on 'the old imperatives' in the altogether sparer sequence 'Songs for the End of the World' and an elegy for Seamus Heaney that will be hard to better for deftness and subtlety. Tom Sleigh is a poet, a real one, and he deserves a bigger readership.

Conor O'Callaghan's third collection, The Sun King *(2013), is published by Gallery.*

THE VULNERABLE BODY

Mona Arshi, Small Hands, *Pavilion, £9.99*
ISBN 9781781381816
Andrew McMillan, physical, *Cape, £10*
ISBN 9780224102131
Kim Moore, The Art of Falling, *Seren, £9.99*
ISBN 9781781722374

reviewed by Julia Bird

. . .

"I taste it because it might taste of honey" begins Mona Arshi's prose poem 'Taster', and continues "I taste it because my brain is a hive. I taste it because I'm properly assimilated. I taste it because I was an only child and I refused to share the oranges in the playground" – and on through a lickable list of possibilities until the neatly tucked-under conclusion, "I taste it because this morning, I saw the first crocus push through the earth and it was yellow. With my tongue I taste it." Arshi maintains this inquisitive omnivorousness throughout her debut collection. *Small Hands* is an invigorating array of tests and experiments by a poet eager to challenge the extent of her skills and subject matter. Odes bunch up next to ghazals next to memoir. The sensualities of big-cat keeping are used to explore a complex interdependent relationship in

'The Lion' ("I tend to his mane and // he sets a thousand scented fuses under my skin"), whereas 'On Ellington Road' is a carefully edited photo album of a West London childhood ("The white-haired lady we called 'Mum' at / number 4, roaming the fenceless gardens, / until they brought her back in"; "My dad, insomniac shift-worker, blood- / eyed, nursing his head in our tiny kitchen"), while 'Mrs M Unravels' is a bleakly surreal comedy monologue:

> 'I don't want to teach you to suck eggs,'
>   I say 'but from where I stand (and I am
> standing pouring out the tea) 'Mrs M,
>
> we share the same enigmatic bone don't we?'

Part Samuel Beckett, part Victoria Wood.

If this rich buffet smacks of sensory overload, then consider instead the book's quiet core: a sequence of elegies for the poet's brother Deepak, to whose memory the collection is dedicated. The taste of them is salt, bitter. "*Could you confirm you were his sister?*" asks 'Phone Call on a Train Journey', a poem which hands the valuables back to the living. His "rimless glasses" returned to her in their "padded sleeve" ache with unprotectable vulnerability. At the end of 'The Urn', the last but one poem in the sequence, we come to realise that the small hands of the book's title are those of the brother – "she's here reimagining / his small hands, his finger-bones". It's a quiet yet imperishable act of remembrance.

The book concludes with another such act – the astonishing 'Ballad of the Small-boned Daughter'. This is the most disquieting revivification of the ballad form I've read in a long time. It's a murder-ballad, the traditional form cracked open to accommodate a disturbing account of the honour killing of an "unwieldy daughter" by her parents:

> 'You are as beautiful my *Jaan*
>   as the words or tears I'll shed'
> as she warmed the blade against
>   her cheek, fine as silken thread.

The daughter was Shafilea Ahmed, whose parents were found guilty of her murder in 2012. Arshi trained as a lawyer and worked for a human rights organisation for many years. The aggregate of her legal and poetic vocations forms the keystone poem to an open-eyed, open-hearted first collection.

Like Arshi's, Andrew McMillan's collection *physical* is a debut. The Selina Chen photo on McMillan's cover is the back view of a young male nude, the model hugging himself so hard his fingers are leaving drag marks in the flesh. This is exactly where the book is situated: the place where exposure and observation of the male body converge, where the flesh is simultaneously mortified and comforted. The muscle-bound bench-pressers and bicep-curlers of 'the men are weeping in the gym' have hearts grown too big for their chests and chests grown too big for their shirts: "they feel / nothing when the muscle tears itself / from itself   that they don't hear / the thousands of tiny fracturings / needed to build something stronger". 'urination' contains a moment of revelatory bodily intimacy as a pair of lovers join hands on the first pee of the morning – "feel the water moving through him and / knowing that this is love   the prone flesh / what we expel from the body and what we let inside". The poem is a display of defencelessness, and the reader is trusted to respond accordingly.

Thom Gunn is undoubtedly godfather to this book. McMillan has written that Gunn's *Collected Poems* was his guidebook for the navigation of his early gay experience. 'Saturday night – a broken cento for Thom Gunn' is half fan letter, half thank you note. Lines from Gunn's own 'Saturday Night' poem set in a '70s San Francisco sauna are cut with an experience that's just as hungry, just as tense, but is firmly located in the here and now: "the night's been drank   the sun is low   the sun / *cannot find strength now for another start*". Wordclots scattered throughout the collection – "strengthofbody", "shortflightstopover", "futurefather" – add a note of Merseybeat, but McMillan's influences are thoughtfully processed and unified, not least by his unpunctuated, uncapitalised style. There's barely a full stop or a capital letter in the book – he controls his argument instead by providing long white pauses as places where we can take a breath. The lowercase lines give the illusion of watching a Messenger conversation scroll by, but a second glance is all that's needed for the careful workings of his lineation to reveal itself.

"An extraordinary debut from a twenty-six-year-old poet" sounds the book's press release, pointedly alerting us to the poet's youth. Readers north of thirty or – heaven forbid – forty may raise an eyebrow at its penultimate poem, 'A Gift'. It's a tender tip of the hat to "the ones I never touched… the ones / who wanted to watch films" and a twenty-one line salute to a roll of others, concluding "for all of them / a gift   we were young   we only had our bodies". This rueful Generation X-er can only counter with a cry of "you still *are* young!" and the observation that these hymns to the body are just as attentive to the intricacies of the mind as to those of the physicality they celebrate.

'How I Abandoned My Body to His Keeping' is a run of seventeen poems in Kim Moore's *The Art of Falling*, a sequence dealing with "the story of a woman embroiled in a relationship marked by coercion and violence". The tone established with the first poem is preacherly, its rhetoric ancient:

And in that year my body was a pillar of smoke
and even his hands could not hold me.

And in that year my mind was an empty table
and he laid his thoughts down like dishes of plenty […]

But subsequent poems twist and turn, each one trying out a new entry point. First person, third person, straight anecdote, spirit animal metamorphosis, end-rhymed lines, lines split with slashes, sestinas. It's not a tale told chronologically either – episodes and thought processes recur, cyclically. "That year my tongue spoke the language / of insects", the first poem ('In That Year') continues, to be followed pages later by the poem titled 'The Language of Insects':

there are spiders that eat one another,
there are ants that follow each other
in a spiral, smaller and smaller […]

The repetitive, multi-perspective effect mirrors the woman's situation – the cycle of violence and calm, the constant questioning of self. "You told me I'd be writing about it / all my life", the title poem of the sequence asserts, and the last poem concludes "I pretend that I've been heard", suggesting that the application of all the poetic technique in the world is not going to be enough to finally get this matter written out and closed down. Recounting a story of this nature requires control of its imprecise and interpretable elements: "he was not black and white / he was nothing like that" from 'He Was the Forgotten Thing'. Occasionally, Moore's control slips and imprecision turns to vagueness – "he was buses roaring past like blind heroes" from the same poem, for example – but overall, this troubling sequence is doing hard work at the heart of her first full collection.

Balancing the troubles of the book is a wonderful series of poems which have sprung from Moore's parallel career as a teacher of brass music. 'Teaching the Trumpet' and 'The Trumpet Teacher's Curse' find a way to write about adult-child relationships outside the parental bond. This can be a liberating position – "a curse on the girl / who stuffed a pompom down her cornet / and then said it was her invisible friend who did it" – or one of compassionate advocacy. "Dear Mr Gove", Moore writes in the poem of that name, "there is also the problem of Matthew who cannot read or write too well but who can play Mary Had A Little Lamb with perfect pitch there is the problem of his smile afterwards". Moore is a poet you'd want fighting your corner, too.

Julia Bird's most recent collection is Twenty-four Seven Blossom *(Salt, 2013).*

NATURAL LIGHT

Annie Freud, The Remains, *Picador, £9.99*
ISBN 9781447271161
Sheri Benning, The Season's Vagrant Light: New and Selected Poems
Carcanet, £9.99
ISBN 9781784101060

reviewed by Fiona Moore

. . .

"Unpromising, deceptive, truncheon-like, rubbery, sexual" –
that's aubergines in the opening poem of Annie Freud's new
collection, *The Remains*. They usually rot on the speaker's worktop but
one evening she fries them, sliced:

> I was Scheherazade, wielding my spatula in ecstasy,
> telling stories to myself, eating discs of melting gold.
>
> ('Aubergines')

Unpromising material for life and art can be turned to gold. Freud's
writing has an ease that makes the reader feel sure-footed. Her language
is zestful and her syntax articulate and orderly. The poems are nearly all
in free verse variously presented. Form suits content; line breaks are

smooth and assured. Occasionally there are end-rhymes. There's very little metaphor line by line but quite a few story-metaphors as above.

According to the blurb, one inspiration for this collection was the broken china Freud dug up from her garden – random shapes and images that prompted voices and which appear on the cover painted (or re-imagined, who knows?) by the author. There's a random, anecdotal feel to *The Remains*. What holds it together is a distinctive tone familiar from Freud's last book *The Mirabelles*, especially the final section, which used letters and conversations with her mother.

Poems in *The Remains*, often dedicated to family and (presumably) friends, enact social discourse of a certain kind. To read them is to be a vicarious dinner-party guest. The talk is of art, food, words English and French, social situations pleasurable or awkward, music, gardens and the English countryside, with an occasional reference to Baudelaire or tango. There's really only one speaker, who is fluently, sometimes poignantly witty about these things to entertain the company, celebrate being alive and make a stay against mortality:

> and she began again *I haven't the*
> and everyone including me
> who loved her
> knew she had it
> even if she no longer knew
> exactly what it was
>   ('Anne Bancroft Addresses the No-Name Ladies' Lunch Club')

The Remains is illustrated by Freud. This works well for 'Forty', a small poem on hatred of numbers, nearly crowded off the page by a fractal proliferation of ferny leaves about which there is something mathematical. 'I, Who Love Chairs' consists of a critique of the Mastermind chair opposite a page-long, world-encompassing list of chosen subjects. A few teasing lines entitled 'Birth Control' are dedicated to Freud's father (Lucian the painter, father of many). 'Homage to de Chirico' reads like an autobiographical account of a brief friendship with the artist in Rome in his late, unsuccessful years. 'Zaluzianskya' imagines a flower name into an extra daughter and/or

> a bold revolutionary girl,
> throwing stones at the totalitarians, telling the truth about everything.

Everyone would have wanted to know you.
[...]
ZALUZIANSKYA!

However well these poems work on their own terms, I'm not struck by anything particularly original in their language, form or subject matter; or attracted by their tone or type of discourse, though that is partly a matter of taste. There's usually little left for the reader to imagine. A few poems stand out because they venture into strangeness. The title poem begins:

Tonight, my subject matter is the Fall of Rome
and I see a purple cloud in the empty street.

At once I think of emperors, Purple Emperors, W.H. Auden, a long-ago lecture theatre and Mastermind. The rest doesn't entirely fulfil the promise of that stately first couplet in a series of intriguing not-quite-non-sequiturs, taking in "slave mentality", fairytale mermaids and princesses, middle-men, a "you" who has succumbed to dull habits, and finally

Every day I drink my coffee from this little cup

I found in a job lot. Beauty, beauty, beauty,
I'd rather die than let go of her.

('The Remains')

"[H]er" is both beauty and the cup, any piece of which might one day resurface in someone's garden. This poem allows readers space to be in doubt and make their own connections. My favourite, 'The Room That Isn't There', does that too (and is also in couplets – coincidence, or page-space to allow the thinking-space?): "it dwells behind the door, a simulacrum / of my mind, my womb, my unlived life, my life to come..."

The Season's Vagrant Light is Canadian Sheri Benning's first full publication in the UK, containing new poems and a selection from her two earlier books. The title, taken from a new poem, is characteristic of her style; her work is full of light and elemental and natural imagery. This is the opening verse of 'The Breath of Looking':

The great horned owl underfeather you found

suspended on brome teaches you about the near
imperceptibility of grief. About thinness.
How light, hardly snared by down,
filters through and changes just-so
and so grief wears you, makes
you its slight shadow.

I veer between enjoyment and scepticism at this: scepticism in reaction to
the statement "teaches you... grief", and enjoyment of the underfeather and
then how the metaphor is unfolded with precision in the last four lines.

Benning's poems are rich in description – perhaps most successful
when it's hard-edged, even viscerally or brutally so, and exercises the senses,
as in the opening of 'What Passes Through': "November sky: a mouth /
that has smoked too much for years." Speaker and poet appear close to
interchangeable in poems that often evoke the mood of a place along with
associated memories and relationships. In '*Magnificat*' the place is an
abandoned cemetery in farm country:

through hanks of ditch grass –

fescue, brome, spear, bluestem, blue-eyed,
hip-high sow thistle, coyote-scat cairns [...]

The poem tells stories of loss and hardship to their source (mother or
grandmother, maybe) – a sister dead from Spanish flu, others stillborn:

Oldest daughter,
you prepared them for the earth,

wiped vernix from fists and eyes. Fetal curled,
washed clean of birth's grease, sebum and cilia,
like the vegetable seeds you steeped to soften husks.

Those last three lines are full of sibilance, ee, f, v, b and p – out loud one
has to speak them slowly, pay them full attention. Some of the most
successful poems address Benning's Saskatchewan farming background,
something she shares with Karen Solie.

Sometimes the description is looser, impressionistic and adjectival.

'Thin Moon Psalm' is a long, fragmentary poem set at a monastery in the New Mexico desert. It begins with couplets, "dizzy moon, thin with sorrow- / light, falls beneath dawn", interspersed with words from the Kyrie. There is some striking language, especially

> Thirst throbs on the dark drum, a fire-flower
> in the mouth cave, syncopated to the snake heat-hum –

though I wasn't quite transported to this astonishing place. Some of the more abstract imagery, including that couplet, made me wonder if Benning reads Paul Celan – who in fact appears on a list of writers she's said she returns to; names range from Louise Glück to Jack Gilbert to Karen Solie and Anna Akhmatova to Tomas Tranströmer.

Benning scores her poems in many ways to bring out their plangent music: short lines, long lines, a mixture, lines out across the page; couplets, tercets, longer verses, prose. Occasionally, this becomes interestingly experimental. Two poems consist of a painting's title followed by a blank page and (prose) footnote – a slant approach that allows something direct to be said:

> 1 The face in the Rembrandt of the man pulling Christ off the cross. It's my father pacing from the machine shed to the barn. Night diffuse with the silence of *I have nothing*. Empty-arm begging of autumn fields beneath sky. Dry snow – flaked stars, moths of reflected light.
> ('*Descent from the Cross*, Rembrandt, 1634[1]')

This longish book places the older poems first and rather densely, without page breaks between them, and new poems at the end. I read *The Season's Vagrant Light* from front to back and thought (on re-reading too) that the newer poems are, on the whole, the strongest. After several readings I still have that veering feeling: a need (perhaps because of too-English tastes) to suspend disbelief for some of the more purple passages, mixed with appreciation for this richly worded record of love, hard landscapes and loss: "the winter riverbed, the long, / slow ache I carry inside" ('That Song That Goes').

Fiona Moore's pamphlet Night Letter *will be published by HappenStance in September 2015.*

GEOGRAPHIES

Steve Ely, Englaland, *Smokestack*, £8.95
ISBN 9780992958145
Tom Pow, Concerning the Atlas of Scotland, *Polygon*, £12.99
ISBN 9781846973017
Peter Riley, Due North, *Shearsman*, £9.95
ISBN 9781848613942

reviewed by David Wheatley

. . .

English identity and its roots can lead poets into dark places. There is a peculiar moment in Donald Davie's *Thomas Hardy and British Poetry* when, addressing the inertia of politics since the Profumo affair, he suggests that anyone disillusioned with the Left should look not to the Conservatives but "much further to the Right". He was writing in 1972, heyday of the National Front. At least Davie never actually killed anyone, unlike Egill Skallagrímsson, poet and murderer, who fought on the English side against the Norsemen in the Battle of Brunanburh. Cross Skallagrímsson's panegyric to King Æthelstan with post-war West Yorkshire via Bunting and Hill and you've got Steve Ely's *Englaland*, a berserker's yawp of a long poem. Since I mention the National Front, they're in here too, bubbling up from the same well of conflict that gives us the striking miners, football hooligans, Falkland veterans, and suicide bombers of the poem's dramatis personae.

One section of *Englaland* is called 'Mongrel Blood Imperium', and at the root of Ely's Albion complex is the confusion hymned by Tennyson: "For Saxon or Dane or Norman we, / Teuton or Celt, or whatever we be!" Often what passes for historical memory is an anachronism we foist on the actual past, as when Philip Larkin discovered that the hand-holding of the couple on his Arundel tomb was the work of a Victorian restorer. A reference in Ely to '*opus anglicanum*' probably owes less to a passion for medieval embroidery than a present-day concern with the work of Geoffrey Hill ("*Opus Anglicanum*, their stringent mystery riddled by needles"); and it shows. I had the experience recently of reviewing another book heavily marinaded in Hill's influence (Toby Martinez de las Rivas's *Terror*), but the parallels in Ely's case – the mythos, the diction ("The King's endowment: lauds in the forest chantry"), the *Mercian Hymns*-like disposition of the prose paragraphs on the page with a hanging indent, are uncanny.

Englaland proceeds by overload and hypertrophe. 'Big Billy', a Beowulf-flavoured boasting song, begins: "Brusson Big Billy, beat-em-all brawler, / bane of bullies and blathering blowhards". Big Billy is boozily good with his fists, then. Twelve pages later, he is still "Beer-balmed, blarneyed, blissfully blotto", but it's the reader who is on the ropes. Peter Reading was another dab hand at pastiche Anglo-Saxon, but also knew how to exploit a certain runic terseness. The blustering style may be a defence mechanism, a deflection of the violence bound up so closely with identity when even watching a football game is tantamount to attending a "Klan rally". 'Scum of the Earth', a play, reminded me of Les Murray's *Subhuman Redneck Poems* in its combination of real and internalised violence, its challenge to and mimicking of genteel condescension. Ely gets into all kinds of minute detail on Irish history in a passage on Morrissey (Steven, not Sinéad), 'Irish Blood, English Heart', behind whose "blood-dipped rose / efflorescing from emerald sepals" I detect a longing for a pre-Reformation unity of culture where the "fire and the rose are one", as Eliot might say.

After so much sound and fury, I found the most durable things in *Englaland* in the lovely closing 'Song of the Yellowhammer', strongly reminiscent of the excellent translations from Rǫgnvaldr Kali Kolsson published by Ian Crockatt as *Crimsoning the Eagle's Claw*. No panacea is found for history's cycles of violence, but it is absorbed into a filigree pattern of memory, a genuine *opus anglicanum* after all:

> Æthelstan, war-wager   waster of wapentakes
>   humbler of hundreds   corpser of kings.
>   Albion passes   to Ælfred's wolf-whelp
>   abaser of armies   Lord of lives and lands.
>   Even the paths   of the Highland deer
>   belong to Ælle's   golden-haired Ætheling.

Writers love maps. "While walking this land, I am the pen on the paper", Tim Robinson has written of Connemara; "while drawing this map, my pen is drawing the land." Tom Pow appears to have done most of the surveying for *Concerning the Atlas of Scotland* not on the ground but in the National Library of Scotland's Bartholomew Archive. From Treasure Island to Joan Blaeu to Sakhalin Island, he fairly covers the territory, riffing on the obligatory Jorge Luis Borges reference (the one-to-one map) as he goes. There is a whiff of the collection-as-residency-project to the writing: Pow lacks the sense of furious engagement with his subject we find in Ely, and is not above slipping into soundbitey nostrums ("maps archive our appetites", "motoring / was about more than getting from A to B"). The self-reflexive 'Silences' gets closer to the spirit of the enterprise, with its meditation on absences from maps ("No, this is not a / mountain. This is memory / waiting for your boots"), and 'The Map' picks up where Elizabeth Bishop left off, painting the encounter of brightly coloured nation states with the danger zones yet to achieve any formal definition.

Some of the most interesting things in the book lurk in the marginal descriptions of Bartholomew maps, such as that of the "Cape Colony showing the distribution of goats" or the 'Map of Scotland to Illustrate Mr Harvie Brown's Paper on the Tufted Duck'. Pow's near-homonym Susan Howe also makes extensive use of archives in her work, but her style involves a closer integration of found material into the narrative (or anti-narrative) thread, with less by way of explanatory framing. In longer poems such as 'The Soviet Map of Edinburgh' and 'The Colourists' the material would benefit from a fractal detour or two off their rather linear path, diegetically speaking. "There's no innocence / even in the idlest musings on a map", 'The Map' wisely declares, but the poems I liked best here were those that relished the guileful nature of writing and memory – the lovely, elegiac 'Loch a' Choire', the sensual 'Orchard', and the ghostly 'Silences'.

Peter Riley was born in Stockport and spent much of his life in Cambridge before a recent move to Hebden Bridge. With this in mind, I detect a punning intent in his title *Due North*. Like Saint-John Perse's *Anabase* this is a book of migrations, tracking its populations of immigrants, soldiers and labourers through an anthropological lens. "*From far*", it begins, taking off from a Housman poem, "human groups moving / over the great grasslands with the herds, [...] footsteps measured in millennia." Like Larkin's 'Here', it follows a slow, cinematic approach to its chosen patch of North, though the similarities end there.

Due North comes in twelve sections or "chapters", many of which follow a sobering trail into the "demographic disaster zones" of the Industrial Revolution. Riley's Northerners are forever at risk of "getting trapped in various enclosures, including thought-traps", of which the concept of the North itself is a prime example. The North as a zone of warmth and community is present too, but narratives of stylised political defeat – the North as beautiful victim – are resisted ("I am not the soul-doctor to a sick civilisation"). The sharp end of politics certainly makes its presence felt though: among the ghosts commemorated is Anna Mendelssohn, also from Stockport, whose involvement in radical politics in the '70s cost her dear. Behind Mendelssohn lurk other ghosts incapable of elegiac individuation, such as the nineteenth-century Irish immigrants dumped in their thousands in cholera pits, Riley's descriptions of which are grimly moving. In this, as in much besides, he reminds me of the ghost cartographies of Hull and Birmingham we find in Peter Didsbury and Roy Fisher. Classical music is important to Riley, and finding an account of Kathleen Ferrier singing Mahler in Manchester's Free Trade Hall I thought of Terence Davies's raptures over Bruckner concerts in the Liverpool of his youth – and his execration of the pop culture that swept that Reithian world away. There's not much pop culture in Riley either, though there are notes like this: "*sčasování*. A term only properly understood by Janáček."

W.J. McCormack has written, in reference to Seamus Heaney, that Irish poetry often faces a choice between politics and community – the truth of the first too hard-hitting to be palatable, the comforts of the second too palatable to be true. Among the achievements of *Due North* is the channelling of narrative through a "we" whose exact identity remains open-ended and mysterious. Riley's North is not a succession of personae taking their turn onstage, but something closer to a "zone of consciousness", in Jeremy Noel-Tod's phrase, producing deep and resonant music across the centuries.

Due North is a difficult collection to quote at less than length, but the penultimate section of prose poems, 'The Ascent of Kinder Scout', is among the best things in the book: "This is your baby-doll soul, acting out your civic rights. My parents died into this, in the long brick terraces of the Manufacturing Districts. I fled, and hovered trembling in the hills." From *Alstonefield* to *Excavations*, *Western States* and *The Glacial Stairway*, Riley has had a busy time of it in recent years. These superb poems are an exemplary act of witness to personal and historical memory.

David Wheatley's Contemporary British Poetry *(2014) is published by Palgrave Macmillan.*

TRESPASSERS

John McAuliffe, The Way In, *Gallery, £9*
ISBN 9781852356309
Kate Bingham, Infragreen, *Seren, £9.99*
ISBN 9781781722435

reviewed by Gregory Leadbetter

. . .

John McAuliffe's fourth collection takes Edmund Spenser as its presiding spirit in its epigraph: "But if that Land be there, quoth he, as here, / And is their Heaven likewise there all one?" McAuliffe's Spenser is the border-blurring traveller from England to Ireland – an Elizabethan counterpoint to his own transition from Listowel to Manchester, through which he feels for and blurs his own borders.

The Way In continues the poetry of witness for which McAuliffe has become known, attending to the quotidian configurations of the poet's life in companionable fashion: "I point out, / or you do (we are natural pointers)" ('Stand-off on Santiago Street') signals the method underlying the verse. At the heart of the book, however, taking its cue from Spenser's 'Colin Clout's Come Home Again', the sequence 'Home, Again' – with that suggestive, distancing comma at its centre – interrogates those patterns, and, like the collection as a whole, subverts easy certainties about where the poet actually is.

For all its touches of humour and affability, the poetry here is watchful – even suspicious – of the world and its appearances. The speaker of 'Stand-off on Santiago Street' wonders whether the business over the road is, "as I think, about everything – a front". That concern with what is or is not the case, beyond the surface – joking, but not really – extends throughout, to people, place, and to poetry itself.

'From Here' employs the interwoven lines of the villanelle to unravel the arbitrariness and inherent instability of boundaries, quietly summoning up the uneasy neighbour-hood of Irish and British history. The legal and political divisions of the border across the lake are both present and absent: "the view from here is the border, / law and order written on water". It is a richly ambivalent piece, politically precise in ways that only poetry can achieve. Elsewhere, the double-edged humour continues to hold in poise "a magpie – the national bird, / opportunist, a noise abroad" ('Soft Landing') with the sense of the "Emigrant, optimist, disowning the borders / we didn't see ranging around us like axe heads, / every word out of our mouths someone else's" ('By Now'). The verse is at its most interesting in these tensions, with their implicit scepticism as to national and personal status – as well as to the status of the utterance that acts upon our mental habitat. The collection's title poem, from the sequence 'Home, Again', presents its defining paradox when it finds "the way out the only way in".

The poetry here feels hungry for answers – another "opaque, glittering" lake yields up a "signal", which remains equally opaque ('Wild') – but does not quite trust poetry to provide them. Several poems stage the processes of writing, as if to interrogate them: 'The Wake' incorporates and reflects on some draft lines, "trying to be straight, / ish, but nothing side-of-the-mouth", while 'The Penny' tries insistently to nip poeticism in the bud: "It's nothing, and don't make it into something, / just a penny, a little coin that wouldn't stick". 'Home, Again' riffs on Spenser's line, "*Then want I words to speak it fitly forth*", with a dialogue on poetry that includes the only clear defence of the art in the book, as "the language drawing us out of ourselves". That's good, but where (comes the doubting voice) does that leave the self? In 'The Red Lion', the opening poem of the 'Home, Again' sequence, the poet considers himself and his friends as they meet in a pub: "Is there something to be said for us, this shower, this avalanche / of poet-critics, pol corrs, stand-ups, lecturers and journalists in verse?" – or does their careerist "online manoeuvring" suggest that poetry itself is "coming to a dying, awful, lazy end"?

It took me a while to *hear* these poems – something in which I see another kind of scepticism at work. In its formalised vernacular, tinged with Audenisms, the verse draws less on the latent music of the language than the abstract joinery of punctuation, syntax and lineation. If Spenser's presence is felt throughout the collection, it is not for those "Spenserian vowels that elope with ease" so beloved of Keats.

That sense of formal resistance – or, perhaps more accurately, wariness of falling into the traps of a poetical manner, as opposed to the authentic thing itself – is at one with the matter-of-factness of much of the poetry: locating, listing, pointing out. Despite the superficially accessible nature of McAuliffe's material, however, the effect – like that signal from the lake – is often curiously opaque or circumlocutory, even in bathos: somehow withholding itself, as if on the cusp of arrival. "Before I say a word, / 'Don't start,' you say" ('Household'), and the reader might wonder if that imperative has become self-chiding, at some level. *The Way In* has an air of deliberate understatement – and yet it is shot through with self-consciousness of its status as poetry. The habit of poetry is clearly ingrained in the life presented here, but I'm left with the sense of a poet questioning what that truly means – and whether that's enough.

In contrast to McAuliffe, the aural texture of Kate Bingham's third collection, *Infragreen*, is powered by the patterns of its 'eloping' vowels – as here, in a speculative description of

> something I want to call our soul,
> alive and fluttering within
>
> as it gets ready to unfold
> the precarious expanding mesh
> of its first full breath into the wings
> you'd hope for of a made-up thing,
> trembling, ticklish and compressed
> as love should be, losing its foothold.
>
>   ('Between Our Feet')

The cumulative musical effect is apt for a collection that brings day-light and dream-light, visible and invisible, into intimate communion. As its title suggests, *Infragreen* aims to carry human vision beyond its habituated range.

Bingham's subtlety is never vague. She most often houses her "made-up things" in the discipline of rhyme, for which she shows her sure feel throughout. A delight in formal effects characterises the book as a whole, with nods to past masters in Hardy and Frost (and a successful cento thrown in to boot). The sonnet is served well, and the villanelle is prominent here, too: a clever pairing of the form in 'Arrangements' is used to serio-comic effect, as each poem undermines the other in coming to terms with paradox and complexity: "for things to stay the same they have to change" says the one; "For things to change they have to stay the same" answers the other. 'The World at One' loosens the villanelle a little more, in ways that show Bingham's skill and confidence in the medium – and as it does, develops a quiet politics of being in response to the horrors and the pressures of the global news media:

> bring me pencil, paper, chewing gum
> and I will stay at home and do no harm,
> imagining myself a world for one
> where what I did was what I should have done.

That implicit concern with the place of the writer in the world – at once querying and justifying the self-justifying ways of the writing life – is complemented elsewhere by a concern with the faith of the artist in her own work. The haunting ballad 'By the River Lau' imagines a lone artisan who finally makes "her masterpiece", an origami man. He seems to come alive in her hand, "the glimmer of a thought behind / his glossy onion eyes", but in "the silkscreen dawn" of the morning after, "a poor, imperfect, woman-made / man shape was all she saw" and – her faith in what he seemed to be gone – she unfolds and thus kills him: "a tiny shattered skeleton / revealed what she had done", and her mind itself unravels. It's an admonitory myth.

Human life and its habitats figure in this collection as a shared garden – not in any twee sense, but as something we transform by our activity, and which transforms us by its own. The opening poem, 'Ultragreen', aligns the poet to the life within and beyond herself, through the lens of a drop of water, and "Something like photosynthesis begins". The mind is left, like the water drop "in the crux of a leaf", "half letting go of itself / half hanging on" ('Infragreen').

Infragreen questions as well as raids the inarticulate, alert to

> the possibility that somewhere
> in the processes of deep non-verbal reasoning

> some filament might signal back
> and the silence between us
> end in words.
>
>   ('Questions')

Nothing is taken for granted in the intellectual universe of these poems: instead they draw strength from going on creating in the face of mystery.

Bingham is faithful to the fugitive spectrum of perception: "Only a state of mind or trick of light, / I tell myself, but no less felt for that" ('Tapetum Lucidum'). In her hands, "A feeling wonders what it might become" ('Rosa Wedding Day') – an instinctive affirmation of William James's sense that "the recesses of feeling, the darker, blinder strata of character, is the only place in the world in which we catch real fact in the making". This gives the collection its metaphysical tact – a rare quality: though perhaps the day is coming when it will be more fully acknowledged as fundamental to the distinctive authority of poetry.

Infragreen is full of sensuous, imaginative and beautifully accomplished work. It succeeds in leading the consciousness beyond its deadened rounds: "why else do you think I'd choose to go // at twilight in the rain if not to listen / to my hairs on end, my senses trespassing?" ('The Wood').

Gregory Leadbetter's Coleridge and the Daemonic Imagination *(2011) is published by Palgrave Macmillan. His pamphlet* The Body in the Well *(HappenStance) appeared in 2007.*

COMPLETE PAYMENT

Paul Durcan, The Days of Surprise, *Harvill Secker, £12*
ISBN 9781846559716
Eiléan Ní Chuilleanáin, The Boys of Bluehill, *Gallery, £9*
ISBN 9781852356217
Peter Sirr, The Rooms, *Gallery, £9.50*
ISBN 9781852356033

reviewed by Patrick Crotty

. . .

Since coming to public attention by way of a 1967 press photograph showing him shyly flaunt a flower in his hair at a Dublin 'happening', Paul Durcan has been one of the most insistent presences in Irish cultural life. Never afraid to look or sound foolish, he has for five decades disguised artistic ambition of the rarest kind under a cloak of cartoonish surrealism and populist gesture. While resourcefully amplifying the tremors generated by the bumpy social and economic evolution of his native southern Irish state, his work has also offered that polity's pre-eminent artistic response to the more vicious turbulence simultaneously rumbling on north of the border. Durcan spent the early decades of his career outside the customary support systems of Arts Council grants and creative writing appointments. In recent years he has been spared starvation by his membership of Aosdána (Charles Haughey's attempted realisation of W.B. Yeats's dream for an Irish Academy of Letters) and his incumbency, from 2004 to 2007, of the cross-border Ireland Chair of Poetry. He has toured with John Cooper Clarke, recorded a single with Van Morrison and held a 'diary' spot on RTE Radio's *Today with Pat Kenny* show. Yet for all its popularity – with Irish sales sometimes competing with Seamus Heaney's – Durcan's poetry has been ignored by the academy, its bristling particularities proving uncongenial to the identity obsessions and associated abstraction worship that subdue thought in English departments. If any contemporary poetry in English confirms Yves Bonnefoy's definition of the art as the antidote to ideology, this is it.

To stress Durcan's contribution to Irish life risks misrepresenting his work, and understating its importance. He's worth reading (and writing about) primarily because of his extraordinary skill in striking lyric fire from "a selection of language really used" by ordinary people in day-to-day situations. His line endings – he generally, though not always, writes free verse – are exquisitely tuned to the cadences of speech and he displays a unique instinct for releasing the visionary possibilities hidden in colloquial phrases. Some of his most memorable poems, in any event, have little to do with Ireland – the responses to paintings in London's National Gallery that make up *Give Me Your Hand* (1994), for example, or 'Give Him Bondi' (from *Cries of an Irish Caveman*, 2001), a subtly allusive, scarifying, comically self-deprecating 556-line narrative of near-drowning in Australia.

The Days of Surprise is Durcan's seventeenth full collection, and one that bears fresh witness to the intensity of the demands he has placed upon himself over the decades. Though they contained wonders, his volumes before *The Berlin Wall Café* (1985) were in some respects ragged and uncertain, their occasional *tours de force* surrounded by underworked or tonally insecure poems in various styles. This new book is notably consistent in quality, the engine of its default mode thrumming reliably to dramatise a series of encounters with characters drawn from a range of backgrounds. Many of the protagonists are caught as it were off-guard, snapped in heart-rending and hilarious poses under the shadow of death. The poet's late mother is a pervasive presence. Among the more vividly painful autobiographical comedies here are 'First Mixed Party' and 'The Poet and the Judge', the latter an anecdote of eyeballing frisson between the author's alcoholically enhanced friend Michael Hartnett and his sober despotic father, Judge Durcan. The hapless child-self of the speaker of the

Paul Durcan © Gerald Mangan 2015

book's opening poem, '57 Dartmouth Square', inhabits a series of power fantasies, being cast in turn as the house of the title and the Messiah:

> The real Christmas Day was the Feast of the Epiphany, 6 January,
> When at long and dear last in the suspenseful chess game of life
> I got to move the Three Wise Men into the Crib.
> At last they had found me and I wriggled in ecstasy.

The fact that Durcan's fantasies recognise their status as such is the source both of the anguish and authority of these poems. In the superb 'Breaking News', the recently departed Seamus Heaney speaks down the chimney to the grieving author:

> 'Are you alright down there, Poet Durcan?'
> (That's how he always addressed me down thirty-seven years –
> 'Poet Durcan')
> 'Calm down, I'm only dead...'
>
> [...]
>
> 'And now I put the key for the first time
> Into the door of my father's house.'

The recall of 'The Blackbird of Glanmore' in that closing pair of lines is a masterstroke, flawless in its tact, deeply enriching, and yet less than essential to the uninformed reader's enjoyment of the text.

Eiléan Ní Chuilleanáin's career, too, goes back more than forty years, though her work has only recently begun to attract the attention it deserves outside Ireland. Ní Chuilleanáin is in many ways Durcan's opposite: reticent, oblique, as adept at slipping under the top as he is at piling over it. If Durcan's poems characteristically seek to embody the solidity of the world, hers resist particularity of time and location, as if distrustful of that same world's claim to substantiality. Many of Ní Chuilleanáin's lyrics have the timelessness of dream or parable. Their cryptic diffidence and reluctance to fully disclose their meanings are frequently underscored by feminine line endings and a refusal of the consolation of rhyme. The first piece in the new collection performs an elaborate withholding of the information promised by its sly title, 'An Information'. Ní Chuilleanáin's elisions and evasions are no mere exercises in whimsy, however, and her lyrics are weighted by an awareness of suffering and injustice (unspecified persecution in 'Who Were Those Travellers', unidentified trauma in 'Witness'). *The Boys of Bluehill* may take its name from a well-known hornpipe and make repeated references to wedding dances but its persistent concern with music (and, indeed, with painting) is far from lighthearted. One of the most haunting poems here, the ekphrastic 'A Musician's Gallery', meditates on the stressful, even tortured balance between spirit and matter necessary to give what it terms "presence" to art and its practitioners:

> Who is listening,

> who can catch the lost bar? The f-shaped hole
> on the cubist violin swallows it up until
> the fiddler's return to haul it out, bend
> her shoulders in a crouch, alert for the signal
> to release the note again, matching
> the wedding racket and the heavenly echo
> calling to the angel to let his own note sound.

Curiously perhaps, Ní Chuilleanáin's own note sounds most resonantly in *The Boys of Bluehill* when she bends her shoulders in a crouch to translate the anonymous ninth-century monologue rendered here as 'Song of the Woman of Beare'. The many existing English versions of this famous complaint against the miseries of age and bodily decrepitude expand on the syllable count of the Old Irish original, thereby lending the poem a plangency and volubility at odds with its gnomic, curt nature. Ní Chuilleanáin opts for an unvaried six-syllable line over thirty-four quatrains. The result is a matter-of-fact economy of expression that grows more unsettling with each reading:

> My right eye was taken
> To buy eternal land
> And now the left eye goes
> To complete the payment.

> The wave at high tide, then
> The tide falling again –

What high tide fills for you
Is emptied by low tide.

The wave at high tide, then
Falling tide that follows:
I know them, I have seen
Full tide and low water.

The wave at high tide – how
Silent my store-house now:
Once I fed multitudes,
A hand fell on them all.

Peter Sirr has been active as a poet and thoughtful reviewer of poetry for three decades, though unlike Ní Chuilleanáin he has plied his critical trade outside the academy. At the centre of his latest collection stands a sequence of thirty-four untitled sonnets or near-sonnets that play with the Italian etymology of stanza as 'room'. Irish poetry has been here before, one might think, by way of Richard Murphy's 1985 sonnet sequence 'The Price of Stone', but one would be wrong. Murphy's approach was straightforwardly architectural, each of his fifty verbal structures representing a building significant in some way to the poet's biography. Sirr takes by contrast a metaphysical attitude, projecting each of his sonnets as an ultimately doomed attempt to build a house that might make us feel at home in the world. A Heraclitian sense of the fluidity of everything is bracingly, memorably communicated in these poems. That it keeps underlining the flimsiness of Sirr's own structures is the melancholy point:

This is the house that Jack lost, that packed up
and slid away, forgetting Jack and everyone else,
the faces, the photographs, breath on the mirrors,
prints on the bed, forgot hands, feet, fingertips
and so removed us that not a crack in the wall or a stain
in the floor remembered anything that came before.

The volume opens with 'The Mapmaker's Song', a witty credo about the challenges of representation, and closes with a twenty-five page encounter between a gloomy, unwell, seen-it-all-before Bertolt Brecht and a post-crash Irish Republic. 'Audience with B.B.' interstitches quotations from Brecht's poems and songs with Sirr's own sardonic commentary to create a work that is not only feisty, politically alert and funny but radically different in kind from everything that precedes it in the book. If Sirr's concluding collage can seem a little *ad hoc* and over-emphatic at times, it nevertheless exudes an energy and joy in incongruity that bode well for the future development of this engaging and undervalued poet.

Patrick Crotty edited The Penguin Book of Irish Poetry *(2010).*

From the Editor

POETRY PRIZES: AN UPDATE

In the Summer 2014 issue, *The Poetry Review* published an article (by Joey Connolly) on the poetry prizes. One of the criticisms that emerged was a lack of transparency about the judging process – specifically about declarations of interest by judges. In the editorial, I recommended that the competitions "need to be run on principles of good practice, with clear rules concerning declarations of interest, and transparency about the process." As a follow up to that, I wrote to the organisers of the three most prestigious prizes – the T.S. Eliot Prize, the Costa Book Awards and the Forward Prizes for Poetry – proposing that they introduce declarations of interest as part of their judging procedure.

It's fair to say that my suggestion met with some resistance. Neither the Costa Awards nor the Forward Prizes have declarations of interest and both are happy with the status quo. Bud McLintock, on behalf of the Costa Awards, writes:

> [I]ntegrity is absolutely vital, both to me personally and as an ambassador for Costa. One of the many strengths of these Book Awards is that not all of our fifteen category judges each year across all five categories necessarily work solely within the literary world, which in itself widens the sphere of influence considerably, and this

is helpful. During the twenty years that I've been Director of the Book Awards, declarations of interest covering a wide variety of different reasons have very occasionally been made either in advance to me or at the judging meeting to everyone present; none has ever proved to be an issue. I am therefore satisfied that the system works as it is and, in the circumstances, have no plans to change it.

Susannah Herbert, on behalf of the Forward Prizes, is equally content. She made the point that the Forward Arts Foundation was a private foundation and did not have the same requirements as a publicly funded organisation:

> Although there is no formalised process regarding declarations of interest, each of the five Forward Prizes judges is expected to be honest, transparent and scrupulously fair. We find that this works well, as does the fact that there are five judges so no one view can prevail without support from at least two others.
>
> It is easy to see that all judges have a history of friendship, influence, professional connections: the best way to deal with this is threefold. Choose your judges with care. Have five of them. Impress upon them the importance of transparency and fairness. If you are comparing us with any other prize, the presence of five judges – at least two of whom are not poets – should be stressed. We could introduce formal declarations of interest but as I have said we don't feel that's necessary.

The Poetry Book Society, which administers the T.S. Eliot Prize, did not initially have any plans to change its procedure. However, that has now changed. Chris Holifield, the director of the PBS, wrote in May to say that they are introducing "a formal process which can be documented on declarations of interest from this year". This is welcome news.

On the subject of declarations of interest, it is worth asking what does constitute a conflict. Literal nepotism is hardly going to arise. It is indeed possible that someone might find themselves sitting in judgement on a sibling, or a spouse or ex-partner. But that is likely to be public knowledge.

However, there are other proximate relationships that frequently arise in the literary world that impede one's impartiality, and these should be declared. It seems to me the most obvious are those:

1. Between editors and authors
2. Between agents and authors
3. Between work colleagues
4. Between teachers and ex-students and 'mentees'

In addition, I'd suggest judges should be at liberty to declare less visible connections that may influence their decisions. Personally, for example, I would not feel comfortable supporting, or for that matter not supporting, a fellow-poet with whom I have a connection that is valuable and longstanding, even if it's not a close friendship.

Such relationships affect not just the final outcome of a prize but the composition of the shortlists. In practice, the pressure on a judge to get a friend or professional colleague onto the shortlist is more common than is the expectation that one would then try to unfairly influence the final result. It's necessary, therefore, that declarations of interest are required at every stage of the judging process.

It's important to emphasise that the opportunity for judges to declare their interests benefits all parties – not least the judges themselves. When undertaking the role, it's useful to be able to say to your friend, colleague, former mentor, "I will have to declare an interest". And it protects friendships and one's professional relations, and indeed one's reputation, to have this publicly recorded. Additionally, as a prizewinner, you would surely feel the honour was tainted if you had a known ally among the judges. One would need pretty thick skin to disregard the reminders that the triumph was suspect. Above all, however, it would greatly enhance the reputation of the prizes as a genuine means to reward achievement. And the organisations that run them would be seen in a better light if the whole debate about 'nepotism' were removed.

It could be argued that the poetry community is such a small, tight network that if everyone were candid about their interests there would be no one left to decide on awards. I have some sympathy with this view. But is the poetry world smaller than, say, that of the Bar Council or the Institute of Actuaries? Yet such bodies presumably seek ways of acting with transparent impartiality. And nowadays is the poetry world in fact so small? When I look above my desk at the shelves of books sent for review, and the array of poetry magazines (not to mention their online counterparts), I see a populous world – one that is spread across the generations, that is ethnically diverse and geographically dispersed. It can seem small perhaps only because organisations look to a familiar roster of people when choosing their panels. And that in turn fosters the perception that it's all a closed shop. No doubt, our current practices sometimes encourage the expectation of patronage and the reciprocation of favours.

I want to emphasise *sometimes*. For the most part, I can say from my own experience that judges act with fairness. They carry out what is a difficult, time-consuming, and often under-rewarded job with integrity and a sense of public duty. But because there have been instances of favouritism over the years, even the impartiality of the most scrupulous people may be questioned. I think the introduction of declarations of interest (and hopefully other organisations will now follow the Poetry Book Society's example) will change the culture. In the meantime, I'd recommend that judges do volunteer declarations of interest, and ask that they be recorded, so that their own personal integrity cannot be compromised.

No doubt the outcomes of competitions and prizes will remain contentious, infuriating – even risible on occasion. Julian Barnes famously described the Booker Prize as "posh bingo". Well, bingo is preferable to a fix – though I'd suggest the unpredictability of the Booker, and its long and short lists, has more to with the variety of readers' preferences than with pure chance. If we could remove the cloud of favouritism from our competitions, then we could celebrate that healthy subjectivity of taste – and view with equanimity and good humour its less explicable consequences.

Letter from Canada

BE AFRAID

Sara Peters

I've spent the month of July pretending to write this letter from Toronto, Ontario, where I live. But I've actually been writing it from Antigonish, Nova Scotia, a town that stops at the ocean, where I was born and grew up. I secretly use Antigonish as my template, and have unfortunately been known to say that my 'interior' (by which I'm afraid I mean 'soul') will only ever exist in relation to Antigonish.

But I'm no expert! I barely know all of Antigonish's street names. Is it possible to be obsessed with a place, and to simultaneously be ignorant of many of its civic or functioning details, of much of what's normally used to gauge the sincerity of an obsession?

Perhaps I want Antigonish's features to always be swimming slightly under my gaze. I want to feel shadowed and menaced by my own ignorance, my inadequate perceptions, my generalising, my gaps and lapses in attention and understanding. I want to be reminded to stay afraid.

I am a thirty-two-year-old white Canadian woman of mostly Scottish and Dutch heritage. I am middle class and I have no health problems and I am cisgender. This is all to say: I have little to fear. Yet fearfulness is the desired condition of my life.

Here is what I fear writing: a lyric essay by a person who has all the attributes listed above; built upon a self-deprecatory narrative; anchored by approved idiosyncrasies of tone and voice; studded with passages about the horror of the body and self; including compelling confessions of the horror of my *particular* body and self; ultimately a missive re: the necessity of self-acceptance and self-love; hopefully prompting identification and revelation from you, and therefore instigating a trust relationship between you and me and therefore, perhaps, making us feel less alone.

My life is privileged and padded, helmeted and small. For example: I am free to be consumed by recipes and exercise. I am profoundly in love. My sense of humour is intact. I am often able to write without first beating myself into hysterical peaks of anxiety. I am largely no longer interested in acrobatic feats of self-loathing and self-punishment. Speaking technically: there is little to fear, other than relentless misogyny and the detritus of my past.

Nonetheless, I am interested in the kind of fear that recognises that the self is (and should remain) an unstable other, able to offer strange bounties, and also able to undermine our control at any time.

But I don't mean to invoke the gauche and dusty trinity of the ego, superego and id. I mean states of fear that acknowledge the unknowability of the self, but also the unknowability of other people, the impossibility of understanding the damage we do to them, their true opinions of us: these are the kinds of fear that should be cultivated with great tenderness.

I mean: fear that can lead to kindness, alertness, empathy, humility. I mean acknowledging that most people are able to lie and dissemble at least as well as I can. Such practices and acknowledgements may feel unstable, but perhaps only in the way that it might feel unstable to live in a country of permanent spring.

In time, each of us will become someone that our current selves would venerate, despise, pity, or be unmoved by. And this process is happening now – in such fine increments as to be invisible. In time, I may scorn the foods, the hours of the day or night, the earrings, the friends, the parts of myself that I now love.

I fear that my love for the person to whom I am married is changing, as I write this. Such change is unstoppable; maybe it's useful. Yet I fear it. I don't want children, and I used to think I felt no fear about this decision. But that's not true: I'm afraid that I will some-day have a spirit and heart that crave children, and a body and mind unable to bear them.

Of course, I will always fear that I am stupid and cruel, boring and fake;

that I wear bad pants; that I should stop buying costume jewellery; that people privately laugh at me; that I perceive interactions inaccurately; that I will never manage to pay off my student loans; that I will spend my life combing through the same boxed set of personal problems; that nothing I have thought unique to my person has ever been or ever will be unique to my person; that I have a dumb walk.

Eventually I will tire of self-improvement, of trying to coax myself into greater honesty/intelligence/creativity/empathy/whatever. I'll get sick of being assertive and 'stating my needs', caring about my friendships and tending to my family. Of vegetables and jogging and sunblock. I will have neither the ability nor the desire to further investigate or refine myself. Meaning, according to my version of things: I will have neither the ability nor the desire to feel fear.

To relax my hold on fear would mean to regress to pseudo-feral adolescence or curdled narcissism. It would mean that I no longer feared hurting or misunderstanding others, that I presumed their pain was fundamentally visible to me, and that I believed I could pre-approve the person I will become.

I am purely afraid when I'm swimming at Malignant Cove, which is the real name of a real beach that's a twenty-minute drive from where I was born. I'm tasting ground-up fish, wedding rings and coins and bottles, picnic remains from one hundred years ago, pulverised human bodies. I am suspended and beset on all sides. I am passive and bloodless, clammy and deboned, borne by waves. I hope to some day feel great affection for that person bobbing around in her cage of fear, that person I used to call me.

Once my fear has dissolved, I would like to leave my life swiftly and mechanically – like the needle on some record players that automatically lifts and returns. As a ghost I'd approach my territorial hauntings with the precision of a wedding planner or an interior decorator: an inexplicable flash here, an impossible ripple there. Once the water reaches the shore there is so little of it left – how quietly it slips over the stones, barely able to cover them.

Sara Peters's first collection is 1996 (Anansi Press, 2013). Her poems featured in the Summer issue of TPR.

CONTRIBUTORS

Mike Barlow's third collection, *Charmed Lives*, was published by Smith/ Doorstop in 2012 • **Jemma Borg**'s first collection, *The Illuminated World*, was published by Eyewear in 2014 • **Harry Clifton**'s *The Holding Centre: Selected Poems* was published by Bloodaxe in 2014. He was Ireland Professor of Poetry from 2010 to 2013 • **Julia Copus**'s latest collection, *The World's Two Smallest Humans* (Faber, 2012), was shortlisted for the T.S. Eliot Prize • **Sophie Collins** co-edits the online journal *tender* • Greg Delanty's latest collection is *The Greek Anthology Book XVII* (Carcanet, 2013), published in the US as *Book Seventeen: Poems* by LSU Press • **James Giddings** is a graduate of MA Writing at Sheffield Hallam. He is the recipient of a Northern Writers' Award in 2015 • **Jodie Hollander**'s pamphlet *The Humane Society* was published by tall-lighthouse in 2012 • **Sarah Howe**'s *Loop of Jade* (Chatto & Windus) is shortlisted for the Forward Prize for Best First Collection • **Phillis Levin**'s fifth collection, *Mr. Memory & Other Poems*, is forthcoming from Penguin in March 2016. She is the editor of *The Penguin Book of the Sonnet* (2001). She lives in New York City • **Tim Liardet**'s most recent collection is *The World Before Snow* (Carcanet, 2015). His *New and Selected Poems* is due from Carcanet • **Michael Longley**'s latest collection is *The Stairwell* (Cape, 2014) • **Helen Mort**'s first collection, *Division Street* (Chatto & Windus, 2013), was shortlisted for the T.S. Eliot Prize • **Katrina Naomi**'s debut collection, *The Way the Crocodile Taught Me*, will be published by Seren in 2016 • **Billy Ramsell**'s second collection, *The Architect's Dream of Winter*, was published by Dedalus in 2013 • **Simon Richey**'s first collection, *Naming the Tree*, was published by Oversteps Books in 2014 • **Ruby Robinson**'s debut collection, *Every Little Sound*, is forthcoming from Pavilion in spring 2016. She lives in Sheffield • **Carol Rumens**'s next collection, provisionally titled *Animal People*, is due from Seren in 2016 • **Julian Stannard**'s next collection, *What Were You Thinking?*, will be published by CB editions in 2016 • **Julian Turner** was a recipient of a Northern Writers' Award in 2014. His fourth collection, *Desolate Market*, is due from Anvil • **Mark Waldron** has published two collections with Salt, *The Brand New Dark* (2008) and *The Itchy Sea* (2011). His third collection will be published by Bloodaxe in 2016.

The Poetry Society
at the Aldeburgh Poetry Festival 2015

Form & Freedom
Saturday 7 November, Britten Studio, 6pm – 6.45pm, £5

The confines of form or the shortfalls of free verse? **Hollie McNish**, **Kei Miller** and **Helen Mort**, all exponents of poetry on both page and stage, address and update the argument. Outbursts and interjections expected from the audience. The Poetry Society's Director **Judith Palmer** chairs.

PLUS: Young Translators
Friday 6 November, Jerwood Kiln Studio, 5pm – 5.15pm, FREE

The Poetry Society's **Young Poets Network** announces the winners of its Young Translators Competition. Mexican poet **Pedro Serrano** comments on the best translations of his poetry from schools in Suffolk, and young people across the UK. Presented by The Poetry Society and The British Council.

The Aldeburgh Poetry Festival, 6–8 November 2015 is at Snape Maltings, Suffolk IP17 1SP. The full programme is available at thepoetrytrust.org/festival/programme. Make sure you visit The Poetry Society stall during the Festival.

ALSO: Aldeburgh Festival Poets on Tour
Monday 9 November, The Poetry Café, London, 7pm, £6/£5

Kim Addonizio and **Tony Hoagland** join **Paul Nemser** for an evening of American poetry. Tickets £6/£5 concs & PS members. tinyurl.com/nv2x4rq or tel: 0207 420 9880.

THEPOETRYSOCIETY

ARTS COUNCIL ENGLAND — Supported using public funding by

National Poetry Competition Events

Join us in Newcastle and Liverpool this November to hear poetry by National Poetry Competition-winning poets

NPC Newcastle

An evening of poetry readings and filmpoems, with **Beverley Nadin**, **Eliot North** and **Tom Weir**.

Thursday 5 November, 7.15pm
Newcastle Centre for the Literary Arts
Culture Lab, Newcastle University NE1 7RU

Tickets £6/£4/£2
Visit ncl.ac.uk/ncla/events or contact
Melanie Birch melanie.birch@ncl.ac.uk
0191 208 7619

NPC Liverpool

Mark Pajak and **Tom Weir** in an evening of readings and discussions exploring writing, competitions and what inspires the creative process. Featuring Ted Hughes Award shortlisted poet **Patience Agbabi**.

Thursday 19 November, 7pm
Bluecoat, School Lane,
Liverpool L1 3BX

Tickets £5/£4
Visit thebluecoat.org.uk
or contact the Box Office
0151 702 5324

THE**POETRY**SOCIETY

Supported using public funding by
ARTS COUNCIL ENGLAND
ARTS COUNCIL ENGLAND

Connect to the power of poetry on your PC, Mac, iPhone or iPad

The Poetry Review

At your fingertips: additional digital version now available

Now you can browse and search The Poetry Review from anywhere in the world

The new digital edition of *The Poetry Review* means you can browse and search the latest issue – and back issues – of the world's finest poetry magazine on your PC, Mac, iPhone and iPad, from anywhere in the world. Here's how you do it...

Add a digital subscription to your membership of The Poetry Society
If you receive *The Poetry Review* as part of your membership of The Poetry Society, then you can also benefit from FREE access to the digital version of *The Poetry Review*. Simply register, using your membership number, at **exacteditions.com/print/thepoetryreview**

Not a member? Add a digital subscription to your existing print subscription
Add digital access to your annual print subscription for just £24.99 per annum. Sign up at **exacteditions.com/thepoetryreview**. For details of institutional subscriptions, allowing universities and colleges to offer multi-user access, visit **exacteditions.com/library/thepoetryreview**.

To join The Poetry Society as a Full Member and benefit from a membership package that automatically includes the digital magazine, visit **poetrysociety.org.uk/membership** or contact Paul McGrane on 020 7420 9881.

And don't worry if you prefer to stick with the print version of the magazine – simply carry on subscribing in the usual way.

THEPOETRYSOCIETY

Supported using public funding by
ARTS COUNCIL ENGLAND

Gayle Cosgrove, OCA Photography student

Becoming a student has given me such a confidence boost. I was 52 when I started the BA(Hons) Creative Writing. I've found the support, and tutor guidance invaluable.

Deborah Riccio
Writing student

Live | Learn | Create

Contemporary courses you can study from home

Open College of the Arts

0800 731 2116
oca.ac.uk

The Poetry Society and Southbank Centre present

National Poetry Day Live

The Clore Ballroom at Royal Festival Hall, London
Thursday 8 October, 1–6pm

> *"The light is
> shattered into gold
> on every cloud, my
> darling, and it scatters
> gems in profusion."*
>
> *Rabindranath Tagore
> 'Light'*

FREE poetry performances from: Liz Berry, Imtiaz Dharker, Karen McCarthy Woolf, GREEdS, John Hegley, Rachel Rooney, Joshua Seigal, Michael Symmons Roberts, Joelle Taylor, R.A. Villanueva & The Young Poet Laureate of London

See poetry in a different light at National Poetry Day Live 2015. Join our free celebration of poetry and spoken-word, programmed by a group of young poetry producers, who will be shining a light on the UK's thriving poetry scene with a showcase of both the biggest and most up-and-coming names in poetry. The afternoon features an array of light-themed performances, workshops, and installations for all ages. Everyone is welcome to be dazzled by our brilliant line-up of poets.

PLUS: Beginning to See the Light, Thursday 8 October, 7.30pm, £8
In a series of newly commissioned poems, Raymond Antrobus, Malika Booker, Holly Corfield Carr, Jane Draycott, Caleb Klaces and Richard Price examine what's illuminated and what stays in the shadows. Commissioned by Jaybird Live Literature and The Poetry Society, in association with Southbank Centre. For details and to book, visit: bit.ly/1JPyBFe, or phone 0844 875 0073.

Find us on Twitter: @poetrysociety • @litsouthbank • #ndplive

THEPOETRYSOCIETY

Guernsey International Poetry Competition 2016

Judged by Ian McMillan

Your poem on the move, on the beautiful island of Guernsey. Want to know more?

www.guernseyliteraryfestival.com:
Competitions, Poems on the Move, Competition Leaflet 2016
Email: poetry@cwgsy.net **Tel:** +44 (0) 7781 163545

 Guernsey Arts Commission

 Browns Advocates — FAMILY LAW SPECIALISTS

 GUERNSEY LITERARY FESTIVAL

The Poetry Review
Autumn Launch, Birmingham

Join us in raising a glass to the latest issue of *The Poetry Review* – and to celebrate our new digital version – with readings from contributing poets **Gregory Leadbetter, Helen Mort, Billy Ramsell** and **Julian Stannard.**

Thursday 29 October 2015
From 6.30pm. Readings from 7pm

Birmingham City University
The Curzon Building (Room C003)
4 Cardigan Street, Birmingham B4 7BD

 Presented with the support of Writing West Midlands

Tickets are free but must be reserved in advance at marketing@poetrysociety.org.uk or 020 7420 9886